AF539908

FINANCING
SMALL SCALE INDUSTRY

FINANCING SMALL SCALE INDUSTRY

Edited by
Dr. Girish Kumar Patra
Dr. Prakash Chandra Misra
Dr. Gouri Sankar Lall

DISCOVERY PUBLISHING HOUSE
NEW DELHI-110002

First Published - 2006

Reprinted - 2015

ISBN: 978-81-8356-058-0

Financing Small Scale Industry

Published by:

DISCOVERY PUBLISHING HOUSE PVT. LTD.

4383/4B, Ansari Road, Darya Ganj

New Delhi-110 002 (India)

Phone: +91-11-23279245, 43596064-65

Fax: +91-11-23253475

E-mail: discoverypublishinghouse@gmail.com

sales@discoverypublishinggroup.com

web: www.discoverypublishinggroup.com

Printed at:

Infinity Imaging Systems

Delhi

Foreword

Tiny water drops cut the stones.

Small efforts make great strides.

The small-scale industrial sector has emerged as a vibrant and dynamic sector of the Indian economy since independence. With the twin objectives of employment generation and capital expansion, the small-scale sector was highly emphasized consistently in all the successive industrial policy resolutions.

The industrial policy resolution, 1948 emphasized cottage and small-scale industries to be particularly suited for better utilisation of local resources and achievement of 'local self-sufficiency' in respect of specific industrial products. 1956 resolution initiated measures to build the competitive strength of small and village industries. In 1966 the small enterprises were classified as undertakings and ancillaries from the angle of fined capital investment volume. In 1977, stress was given on wider dispersal of cottage and small industries in the rural areas and small towns, and district industries centres (DICs) were floated out to augment the service facilities to small industries. In 1980 ancillarisation and creation of nucleus plants were given emphasis while in 1990 stress was laid on contribution of the sector in over-all exports, employment generation and dispersal of industries in rural areas. In 1991 emphasis was laid on promotion and strengthening of small, tiny and village industries. A new scheme of integrated infrastructure development for SSIs with the participation of State Governments and Financial Institutions and a proactive role of NGO sector was initiated besides effecting changes in investment limits and equity participation. During 1997 the implementation of the recommendations of Abid Hussain Committee raised the capital limit of tiny and small units by 5 times and the ancillary by 4 times, providing a born for enlargement of the small scale sector. In 2000, the limit was down sized by 2/3 for small units and ancillaries fining the limits at Rs. 1 crore and the limit for tiny units being retained at Rs. 25 lakhs.

In 50 years span the numerical growth of the small enterprises was more than 32 lakhs in 2000 AD from 16,000 in 1950 AD. With the thrust of maximisation of output from limited capital investment, the sector has given way to traditional ventures, export promotions, innovations and economic equity.

In the post-liberalisation scenario the historical trend of the small-scale sector has not changed. It has consistently maintained higher rate of growth compared to the total industry sector. Downsizing in the extent of growth compared to the pre-liberalisation period is attributed to the general recession in the industry and economy. In the economic reform process the small-scale sector is not at the receiving end. However, DIVERSITY is highly required in the sector to maintain the progress in the WTO regime.

To face the challenges ahead the sector has to be vibrant with appropriate information network. Small Enterprises Information and Resource Centre Network (SENET) have come into operation w.e.f. April 1997 with a view to pioneer, create and promote data base and information services and facilitate information sharing among the seekers and providers of information and between supportive institutions in mutually beneficial and cost-effective manner. Website *www.smallindustryindia.com* is a valuable backup to march ahead.

Considering the immense potentialities of the Small Scale Sector in the overall backdrop of Indian economy a natural level seminar was organised with the support of UGC. Thought provoking and highly illuminating papers were presented embracing a wide spectrum of issues revolving round the small-scale sector in the country. Those are clubbed together to put forth the viewpoints for reference to thinkers, policy makers, planners, and academicians.

It is sincerely hoped that the proceedings of the seminar will provide fund for thought for those who are eager to see the small sector taking its right position, by moving in right direction and proving its worth in the global boundary.

The efforts of Dr. Prakash Misra in this regard are highly commendable.

—Dr. G.P. Acharya

Contents

List of Contributors

1. **Prof. P.K. Sahu**
   Senior Professor, P.G. Dept. of Commerce,Berhampur University, At present the Vice-Chairman, State Planning Board, Orissa Secretariat, Bhubaneswar-1

2. **Prof. P.C. Tripathy**
   Senior Professor, P.G. Dept. of Commerce,Utkal University, At present the Chairman, P.G. Council, Utkal University, Bhubaneswar-4

3. **Dr. Prakash Ch. Misra**
   Reader in Commerce, Berhampur University, Berhampur-760007

4. **Dr. Ashok Kumar Mohanty**
   Reader in Commerce, Berhampur University, Berhampur-760007

5. **Dr. Girish Kumar Patra**
   Sr. Lecturer, in Commerce, Kendrapara College, Kendrapara

6. **Mr. Prafulla Chandra Mahapatra**
   Reader in Commerce, Rajsunakhela College, Khurda

7. **Dr. Brajabandhu Padhiari**
   Sr. Lecturer in Commerce, Nayagarh College, Nayagarh

8. **Dr. Shyama Charan Acharya**
   Sr. Lecturer, in Commerce, Panchyat College, Baragarh

9. **Dr. Sanjay Ku. Satapathy**
   Faculty member, Dept. of Commerce, R.D. Women's College, Bhubaneswar

10. **Prof. G.P. Acharya**
Professor in Commerce, Retired Principal, Ravenshaw (Autonomous) College, Cuttack-3

11. **Mr. Prafulla Chandra Mohanty**
Sr. Lecturer in Commerce, Aska Science College, Aska, Ganjam

12. **Dr. S.B. Tripathy**
Reader in Commerce, Ravenshaw College, Cuttack-3

13. **Dr. Bijoy Kumar Dash**
Reader in Commerce, Institute of Management & Information Technology, Cuttack-3

14. **Mr. Deepak Kumar Mohanty**
Sr. Lecturer in Commerce, Salipur College, Salipur

15. **Mr. Bana Bihari Mohanty**
Sr. Lecturer in Commerce, Salipur College, Salipur

16. **Mr. Pradeepta Kumar Samanta**
Research Scholar, Berhampur University

17. **Mr. Ch. P.K. Das**
Reader in Commerce, P.N. College, Khurda

18. **Mr. D.K. Mohanty**
Sr. Faculty Member, Nimapara College, Nimapara

19. **Dr. B. Behera**
Sr. Lecturer in Commerce, Ekmra College, Bhubaneswar

20. **Sri Sudhansu Kumar Das**
Lecturer in Commerce, S.G. College, East Jajpur

21. **Dr. Bimal Prasad Nanda**
Reader in Commerce, Govt. College, Anugul

22. **Mr. Ramesh Chandra Jena**
Sr. Lecturer in Commerce, Kendrapara College, Kendrapara

23. **Dr. Pitabasha Mohanty**
Sr. Lecturer in Commerce, Kendrapara College, Kendrapara

24. **Dr. R.K. Nanda**
Reader in Commerce, SCS College (Autonomous), Puri

25. **Dr. Biswanath Dhal**
Sr. Lecturer in Commerce, R.D. Women's College, Bhubaneswar

26. **Dr. A.C. Patra**
Sr. Lecturer & Head, Dept. of Management, State Polytechnics for Women, Bhubaneswar

27. **Mr. M. Bhima Rao**
Sr. Lecturer in Commerce, P.N. College, Khurda

28. **Dr. R.K. Nanda**
P.G. Dept. of Commerce, SCS College, (Autonomous), Puri

29. **Mr. Sambit Mishra**
Lecturer in Commerce, Kendrapara College, Kendrapara

30. **Mr. Bhagabata Behera**
Jr. Lecturer in Commerce, Bhadrak College, Bhadrak

31. **Sri C.R. Panda**
Sr. Lecturer in Commerce, P.N. College, Khurda

32. **Dr. K.B. Das**
Sr. Lecturer in Commerce, P.N. College, Khurda

33. **Dr. Bhagaban Das**
Senior Faculty, P.G. Department of Commerce, Dhenkanal College, Dhenkanal

34. **Dr. Nisha Jain**
Faculty Member, Dept. of Commerce, R.D. Women's College, Bhubaneswar

35 **Dr. Gouri Sankar Lall**
Faculty Member, Dept. of Commerce, Berhampur University, Berhampur-760007

36 **Dr. Sachinadanda Patro**
Sr. Lecturer in Commerce, Hinjilicut College, Ganjam

1

OSFC

The Regional Leader in Financing SSIs

Prafulla Ch. Mohapatra*

Brajabandhu Padhiary**

Introduction

Realising the increasing dependence on traditional agriculture where, marginal productivity appears to be negligible, creation of employment opportunities in the non-farm sector engaged the attention of the Govt., more importantly, in the small-scale sector which has the ability to exploit the local resources effectively, to raise the incomes of the vast rural masses thereby improving their general living standards and above all, to help curbing the regional imbalances in the over all economic development. Orissa, being endowed with all regional imbalances in the over all economic development. Orissa, being endowed with all sorts of natural resources, presents a paradoxical picture of "poverty amidst plenty". The small industries are ideally suited to the developing economy of India with special relevance to Orissa not because of any sentimental or ideological considerations but as purely economic and social compulsion.

---

* **A Faculty Member, Department of Commerce, Rajsunakhala College, Rajsunakhala.**

** **A Faculty Member, Department of Commerce, Nayagarh College, Nayagarh.**

The development of small-scale industry is the aggregate result of combined inputs of technological skills, labour, finance and managerial efficiency. In the process of development, the non-availability of timely and adequate finance generally acts as a severe restraining factor. Finance, therefore, generally assumes a very great importance in the development of small-scale industry.

With a view to ensuring free flow of adequate finance to the small-scale sector, various institutions have been set up along the lines envisaged in the Industrial Policy Resolutions and the five year plans both by the Central Govt. and the state Govt.

In this paper, OSFC as a financing institution in the state of Orissa has been highlighted with special emphasis on its financial assistance to and the development of the small-scale industries in Orissa.

SSIs IN ORISSA: Growth and Present Status

The Government of Orissa, in its Industrial Policies announced from time, has emphasised the need and made provisions for favourable growth of SSIs in the State. The Industrial Policy, 1996, formulated in the context of the ongoing economic liberalisation, reflects the state Government's commitment to growth and development of industries. The objectives of the said policy, inter alias, are to exploit available natural resources, generate employment opportunities through industries like small-scale industries, village and cottage industries, sericulture, handloom and handicrafts and strengthen and upgrade entrepreneurial skills. Table - 1.1 shows the growth and present position of SSIs in Orissa.

OSFC: The Genesis

As the Industrial Finance Corporation of India (IFCI), being the first of its kind for industrial financing at the national level set up in 1948, had limited scope and meeting the financial requirements of small-scale industries was beyond its purview, thus it was felt that financial institutions should also be set up in each state to provide sufficient finance to medium and small-scale industries for promoting industrial development in their respective states. Ultimately, the Orissa State Financial Corporation (OSFC) was established on the 20th March, 1956 by virtue of the State

Table—1.1 Growth and Present Position of SSIs in Orissa

Sl.No.	Year	SSIs set up		Investment		Employment	
		Nos.	Growth over previous year	In crore	Growth over previous year	No of persons	Growth over previous year (%)
1.	1994-95	47,104	–	729.58	–	3,36,781	–
2.	1995-96	2,507	–	74.82	–	13,019	–
3.	1996-97	3,098	123.57	104.53	139.71	15,629	120.05
4.	1997-98	3,186	102.84	134.09	128.28	16,716	106.96
5.	1998-99	3,184	99.94	190.06	141.74	16,776	100.36
6.	1999-2000	3,473	109.08	162.94	85.73	18,608	110.92
	Total	62,552	–	1,396.02	–	4,17,529	–

Source: Economic Survey, Orissa - 2000 - 2001.

Financial Corporation Act in 1951 passed by the Govt. of India. At present there are eighteen such SFCs in the country.

Object and Scope

In conformity with the main object of providing medium and long term credit to the small and medium scale industries in the state of Orissa, its financial assistance could be intended for the construction of factory building, purchase of plant and machinery and renovation and modernisation of existing plant and machinery.

Since its inception, the OSFC has been providing financial assistance for ventures in areas like transport, hotels, nursing homes and clinics and for acquisition of mining and road construction equipments etc. The corporation receives financial assistance from the state Govt. and central Govt. and provides soft loans and margin money for rehabilitation of sick industrial units. Financial assistance to no-industry and backward districts is being considered with due importance in recent years by the OSFC. Besides, the OSFC acts as an agent of the state Govt. for disbursement of capital investment subsidy and soft loans to eligible industries.

Trends in Assistance to SSIs

To assess the financing trends of the OSFC in the development of the small-scale industries in the state of Orissa, it is considered relevant to focus on the following aspects.

(a) Growth trend in sanctions;

(b) Growth trend in disbursements;

(c) Sector-wise cumulative sanction and disbursement up to 31.3.2000;

(d) Sub-sectorwise sanctions and disbursements along with generation of employment opportunities in the small scale sector up to 31.3.2000;

(e) District-wise achievement of sanctions and disbursements of loans with special reference to backward and no-industry districts up to 31.3.2000; and

(f) Recovery performance of OSFC.

Detailed discussion on each of the above is made hereunder:

(a) Growth Trend in Sanctions

Financial sanctions to the small-scale industries by OSFC during a period of last five years from 1995-96 to 1999-2000 reveal that there has been a decline in both the number of units assisted (312) and the amount sanctioned (Rs. 43.74 crore) during the year 1989-99. However, during the year 1999-2000 there has been an appreciable increase in the number of units to 731 as well as in the sanctioned amount to Rs. 72.15 crore. The growth in number of units and amount represents 234% and 165% respectively over the previous year 1998-1999 (Table - 1.2) For the decline in the sanction during 1998-99, Annual Report 1998-99 of the OSFC justifies that "the severe heat wave immobilised the people and brought all the economic activities to a grinding halt for about two months. All these affected the performance of the corporation".

Table—1.2 Growth Trend in Sanction of Loan to SSIs (1995-96 to 1999-2000)

(Rs. in Crore)

Year	*Sanction of Loan*			
	Nos.	*Amount*	*Growth in % over previous year*	
			No.	*Amount*
1995-96	180	27.50	–	–
1996-97	221	32.04	122.8	11.650
1997-98	357	55.98	161.5	174.72
1998-99	312	43.74	87.74	78.14
1999-00	731	72.15	234.3	164.95

Source: OSFC Annual Reports, 1997-98 to 1999-2000.

(b) Growth Trend in Disbursements

Like sanctions, the period of disbursal of loans to small-scale industries covers 5 years from 1995-96 to 1999-2000. It is observed that the corporation has also decreased its disbursement in 1998-99 to 197 units amounting to Rs. 25.60 crore from 279 units amounting to Rs. 29.56 crore respectively in 1997-98. The fall in terms of units assisted and the actual amount disbursed is reduced to 71% and 87% respectively in 1998-99 over 1997-98. During 1999-2000 there has been a jump in assistance both in units (418) as well as in the amount of disbursement (Rs. 33.09 crore) indicating increase of 212% and 129% respectively. The slowdown in the pace of sanctions also influenced the disbursement (Table - 1.3).

Table—1.3 Growth Trend in Disbursal of Loan to SSIs (1995-96 to 1999-2000)

(Rs. in Crore)

Year	*Disbursal of Loan*			
			Growth in % over previous year	
	Nos.	*Amount*	*No.*	*Amount*
1995-96	225	20.52	–	–
1996-97	253	37.36	112.5	182.06
1997-98	279	29.56	110.3	79.12
1998-99	197	25.60	70.6	86.60
1999-00	418	33.09	212.2	129.25

Source: OSFC Annual Reports, 1997-98 to 1999-2000.

(c) Sector-wise Cumulative Sanctions and Disbursements

Since inception up to 31.03.2000, the Corporation has sanctioned loans to 44,168 units amounting to Rs. 1,05,853.85 lakh, out of which effective sanctions to small-scale industries including tiny sector, ancillaries etc are Rs. 57,613.16 lakh (54.4%) followed by transport sector Rs. 25,079.12 lakh (23.7%) and others Rs. 23,161.57 lakh (21.9%). Total number of small-scale units of 30,316 accounting for 68.6% of all units sanctioned till that date. As regards cumulative disbursements till 31.03.2000, both in terms of units and amount of assistance, small-scale sector occupies the highest position. Out of total number of units 25,439, small-scale industries are 14,871 accounting for 58.5%. Similarly out of total disbursed amount of Rs. 92,311.63 lakh an amount of Rs. 51, 215.71 lakh have been disbursed to the small-scale sector accounting for 55.5% of the total disbursal. This indicates the fact that the corporation has been encouraging the growth of industries more in the small-scale sector than other in the state (Table -1.4).

Table—1.4 Cumulative Effective Sanction and Disbursal of Loans as on 31.3.2000

Sl. No.	*Sector*	*Effective Sanction*		*Disbursal*	
		Nos.	*Amount*	*Nos.*	*Amount*
1.	Small Scale Industries (including Tiny Sector, Ancillaries and other SSIs)	30,316 (68.6)	57,613.16 (54.4)	14,871 (58.5)	514,215.71 (55.5)
2.	Transport	11,133 (25.2)	25,079.12 (23.7)	8,458 (33.2)	22,838.47 (24.7)
3.	Others	2,719 (6.2)	23,161.57 (21.9)	2,110 (8.3)	18,257.45 (19.8)
	Total	**44,168 (100)**	**1,05,853.85 (100)**	**25,439 (100)**	**92,311.63 (100)**

Note: Figures in brackets indicate percentage to total.

Source: OSFC Annual Report, 1999-2000.

(d) Sub-sectorwise Sanction, Disbursement and Employment Generation

Industry-wise sub-division in the small-scale sector in respect of sanctions disbursements and employment generation position as on 31.03.2000 reveals that out of the cumulative sanctions made to 9,360 units, 6,066 units (65%) in the handloom industrial sector being the highest followed by 1,646 units (18%) in the tiny sector but as regards the amount sanctioned Rs. 2,401.90 lakh in to tiny sector tops the list with Rs. 1,355.31 lakh (56%) followed by the powerloom units with Rs. 540.61 lakh (22%). In respect of disbursement, out of the total 8,250 units, handloom industry constitutes 5,353 units (65%) and ranks the first position followed by 1,332 units (16%) in the tiny sector. In the total disbursal amount of Rs. 1,958.08 lakh, tiny sector has availed the lion's share of Rs. 1,039.23 lakh (53%) followed by powerloom units with Rs. 513.23 lakh (26%). Coming to the employment generation, out of the total number of 32,816 persons, 16,059 persons (30%) in the powerloom sector. Tiny sector has provided employment to 4,180 persons (13%) and occupied the third place (Table - 1.5). It is clear from the above that traditional handloom sector in the state's economy still has the greater ability to generate more employment opportunities which need to be further strengthened on the financial front.

Table—1.5 Cumulative Sanction, Disbursement and Employment Generation in Village and Small Industries (As on 31.03.2000)

Sl.No.	Sub-sector	Sanction		Disbursement		Employment Generated
		No.	Amount	No.	Amount	Nos.
1.	Handloom Industry	6066 (64.8)	367.41 (15.3)	5,353 (64.9)	321.86 (16.4)	16,059 (48.9)
2.	Powerloom	1,032 (11.0)	540.61 (22.5)	979 (11.9)	513.23 (26.2)	9,790 (29.9)
3.	Khadi & Rural Industries	523 (5.6)	11.15 (0.5)	513 (6.2)	10.13 (0.5)	2,565 (7.8)
4.	Tiny Sector	1,646 (17.6)	1,355.31 (56.4)	1,332 (16.1)	1,039.23 (53.1)	4,180 (12.8)
5.	Handicrafts	46 (0.5)	9.13 (0.4)	39 (0.5)	7.86 (0.4)	78 (0.2)
6.	Sericulture	24 (0.3)	22.75 (0.9)	13 (0.2)	11.19 (0.6)	39 (0.1)
7.	Coir industries	23 (0.2)	95.54 (4.0)	21 (0.2)	54.58 (2.8)	105 (0.3)
	Total	**9,360 (100)**	**2,401.90 (100)**	**8,250 (100)**	**1,958.08 (100)**	**32,816 (100)**

Note: Figures in brackets indicate percentage to total.
Source: OSFC Annual Report, 1999-2000.

(e) District-wise Analysis of Assistance with Reference to Backward Areas

In the line with the priorities attached to the development of backward areas as envisaged in the industrial policy Resolution, 1996 of the Govt. of Orissa, it has been obligatory on the part of the OSFC to extend financial assistance to units set up in those areas. To assess the achievements of the corporation in this direction, district-wise figures in respect of effective sanctions and disbursements up to 31.03.2000 have been chosen. In the order of industrial development, total 30 districts of state have been classified into three categories - 10 nos. backward districts, 6 nos. as no-industry districts and 14 nos. as other districts.

So far as the sanctions to the SSI units are concerned, 30,310 units in toto have been sanctioned as 30 31.03.2000 comprising 6.037 units (20%) in backward districts, 3,577 units (12%) in no-industry districts and 2,06,96 units (68%) in other developed districts. Both backward districts and no-industry districts taken together have 9,614 units which account for 32% of the total units sanctioned. As regards the amount sanctioned, other districts account for 69% of the assistance with Rs. 39,532.26 lakh out of the total of Rs. 57, 613.16 lakh. Sanctioned amount to backward districts was Rs. 4, 296.43 lakh (16%) and to no-industry districts was Rs. 8, 784.47 lakh (15%). In respect of disbursements, out of total of 14,871 units there were 9,899 units (67%) in other districts, 1,781 units (12%) in no-industry districts and 3,191 units (21%) in backward districts. Of the total disbursal amount of Rs. 51, 215.71 lakh Rs. 34, 887.96 lakh (68%), Rs. 8, 746.08 lakh (17%) and Rs. 7, 581.67 lakh (15%) were disbursed to other districts, no-industry districts and backward districts respectively. Total amount disbursed to both backward districts and no-industry districts constitutes Rs. 16, 327.75 lakh (32%). (Table - 1.6).

It is observed that in terms of sanctions and disbursements, other districts enjoy lion's share, probably due to their better infrastructures, which need to be improved in backward and no-industry districts as well, so as to attract more investments for industrial development. The state Govt. no doubt, has laid emphasis on infrastructure development in those areas in its Industrial Policy Resolution, 1996 inviting investments from within and outside the state.

Table—1.6 District-wise Achievement of Loans Sanctioned and Disbursed by OSFC to SSIs (As on 31.03.2000)

		Sanction (Effective)		*Disbursement*	
Sl. No.	*Districts*	*Nos.*	*Amount*	*Nos.*	*Amount*
1	*2*	*3*	*4*	*5*	*6*
A	**Backward District**				
1.	Anugul	360	477.08	197	366.44
2.	Dhenkanal	1,512	1,386.91	725	1,246.02

(Table Contd...)

1	2	3	4	5	6
3.	Kalahandi	415	1,118.40	300	955.34
4.	Naupada	43	86.29	42	95.34
5.	Keonjar	368	1187.67	298	858.06
6.	Koraput	756	1752.11	428	1,1227.34
7.	Malkangiri	205	117.66	110	57.99
8.	Nawarangpur	376	424.05	124	311.84
9.	Rayagada	153	876.05	129	510.22
10.	Mayurbhanj	1,849	1,870.21	838	1,953.08
	Sub-Total (A)	**6,037** **(19.22)**	**9,296.43** **(16.14)**	**3,191** **(21.46)**	**7,581.67** **(14.81)**
B.	**No-Industry District**				
11.	Balasore	1,593	5,315.97	708	5,354.25
12.	Bhadrak	184	846.08	164	828.53
13.	Bolangir	1,146	1,993.23	587	1,917.07
14.	Sonepur	88	2.62	81	14.52
15.	Phulbani	436	526.31	152	514.54
16.	Boudh	130	100.26	89	120.17
	Sub-Total (B)	**3,577** **(11.80)**	**8,784.47** **(15.25)**	**1,781** **(11.98)**	**8,746.08** **(17.07)**
C.	**Other District**				
17.	Cuttack	8,334	9,143.89	1,805	8,512.04
18.	Jagatsinghpur	2,384	902.21	1,813	747.80
19.	Jajpur	211	2,193.15	100	1,511.34
20.	Kendrapara	1,932	669.91	759	618.07
21	Ganjam	1,178	2,745.30	715	2,436.91
22.	Gajapati	33	417.38	37	207.42
23.	Puri	649	1,309.86	624	1,020.34
24.	Khurda	1,997	10,307.04	1,590	911.99
25.	Nayagarh	1,512	1,359.15	1,033	891.31
26.	Sambalpur	706	2,252.33	212	1,813.92
27.	Baragarh	263	679.61	250	563.29
28.	Deogarh	34	150.66	40	164.81

(Table Contd...)

1	2	3	4	5	6
29.	Jharsuguda	78	514.14	74	393.89
30.	Sungargarh	1,385	6,887.63	847	6,094.83
	Sub-Total (C)	**20,696 (68.28)**	**39,532.26 (68.61)**	**9,899 (66.56)**	**34,887.96 (68.12)**
	GRAND TOTAL (A + B + C)	**30,310 (100)**	**57,613.16 (100)**	**14,871 (100)**	**51,215.71 (100)**

Note: Figures in brackets indicate percentage to total

Source: Compiled from Economic Survey, 2000-2001, Govt. of Orissa and OSFC Annual Report, 1999-2000

(f) Recovery Performance of OSFC

Better recovery of loans on the part of OSFC is not only vital for its improvement in the profitability but also it can strengthen its financial viability, and more funds can be made available to improve its financing pattern. During the last five years from 1995-96 to 1999-2000, over all recovery trend reveals that in first three years, it was improved from Rs. 76.77 crore in 1995-96 to Rs. 120.06 crore but in 1998-99 it was reduced to Rs. 110.12 crore which was further reduced to Rs. 101.41 crore in 1999-2000. This may be attributed to the effects of the economic situation prevalent in the country and consequently its adverse impact on the state. For the decline, particularly in 1999-2000, the Annual Report, 1999-2000 of OSFC states, "The reason of such negative trend in recovery was mainly due to devastating cyclone causing serious damage to most of the industrial units. The entire economy remained at stand still for at least 2 - 3 months. (Table - 1.7).

Table—1.7 Recovery Performance of OSFC

Year	*Amount*	*Growth over previous year %*
1995-96	76.77	–
1996-97	112.42	146.44
1997-98	120.06	106.80
1998-99	110.12	91.72
1999-00	101.41	92.09

Source: OSFC Annual Report, 1999-2000.

Conclusion and Suggestions

Industrial financing in the state is the prime responsibility of the OSFC as it is assigned with the tasks for the promotion, improvement and development of industries in the state. Although in the changed circumstances, there are many other agencies catering to the long-term requirements of small scale industrial units, OSFC still continues to be one of the major sources of finance to small-scale industries. In the light of the above discussion, it could be claimed that OSFC has been by and large successful in the industrial development of the state through the promotion of SSIs thereby in fulfilling the assigned role. In this context, the study, made by Dr. P.C. Tripathy (1997) to find out the impact of various financial services (includes OSFC) on industrialisation in the state based on the data for a period of twenty years, is worth quoting, which concludes that "the OSFC with its liberal schemes of financial assistance has been able to create a favourable investment climate in the state. Empirical results revealed that the financial incentives provided by OSFC has significantly influenced gross output from industrial sectors."

To sustain its viability in fulfilling its objectives, the OSFC should be very careful with a close look to the growing incidence of sickness, particularly in the small-scale sector which has become a common phenomenon. The recent amendments to the SFC Act in 2000 are expected to revitalise the corporation with their wide-ranging impact.

In view of the likely order of assistance to the small-scale sector in the light of new industrial policy of the state Govt., it would be necessary for the OSFC to continue to play the role of an important purveyor of term credit to the small-scale sector, particularly to the self-employed entrepreneurs and units in backward areas. To put it in nutshell, OSFC has to ensure that its activities are "Plan-oriented, priority-mined, time-tested and socio-economic-motivated."

REFERENCES

1. Vasant Desai (1986), *Management of Small Scale Industry;* Himalaya Publishing House, New Delhi.
2. P.K. Dhar (2000), *Indian Economy, Its Growing Dimensions;* Kalyani Publishers, Ludhiana.

3. Gopal Swaroop (1986), *Advances to Small Industries and Small Borrowers*; Sultan Chand & Sons., New Delhi.

4. *Economic Survey*, 1999-2000, 2000-2001, Govt. of Orissa.

5. *Souvenir* (1981-82), Orissa State Financial Corporation, Cuttack (Silver Jubilee Year)

6. *Annual Reports*, OSFC, Cuttack (Different issues)

7. Dr. P.C. Tripathy (1997), "Interplay Between Financial Services and Industrial Development Orissa's Experience"; *Contemporary Issues in Financial Services*, P.G. Dept. of Commerce, U.U. BBSR.

8. Nafees Baig & Mohd. A.Ali Khan (1990), *Entrepreneurship and Business Environment*; Ashish Publishing House, New Delhi.

2

Institutional Finance to SSIs in Orissa

A Study of O.S.F.C

Pradeepta K. Samanta*

Ashok K. Mohanty**

Introduction

The Small Scale Industrial (SSI) sector has emerged as the most vital and dynamic sector of the Indian economy. Today it accounts for 80 per cent of country's industrial employment, 40 per cent of total manufactured goods, 35 per cent of country's exports and produces nearly 6000 items[1]. Going by the experiences of developed countries like Japan, USA, China, Korea etc., the small and medium enterprises (SMEs) would continue to remain as the powerful instrument of economic growth even in the era of unprecedented technological revolution and globalisation. In India, during the post-reform era while the large and medium scale grew at 6 per cent p.a., the growth rate in the SSI Sector was 18 per cent p.a.[2]. It is a well known fact that industrial activity is critically dependent on finance. Besides providing term finance, State Financial Corporation (SFCs) formed under SFC Act 1951, are supposed to promote SSI culture in various states of their operations. Since its inception in 1956 the Orissa State Financial Corporation (OSFC) had been financing a wide varieties of industrial/business activities relating to food, textiles, mining, metals, chemicals, cement,

---

* **Mr. Pradeepta K. Samanta, Research Scholar.**

** **Dr. Ashok K. Mohanty, Reader & Head, Department of Commerce, Berhampur University, Berhampur, (Ganjam) Orissa.**

hotel, tourism etc. in the small and medium scale sector. As a sequel to Govt. of India's economic reform programmes, the State of Orissa is also geared up to make it an attractive investment destination. In the backdrop of Govt. of India's New Industrial Policy (NIP-91), the State government formulated its New Industrial Policy in August 1992 and again reformulated its Industrial Policy in March 1996 with a view to improving investment climate for rapid industrialisation and economic development of the State. In the new emerging scenario, OSFC has also stepped up its financial assistance to SSI sector as well as to backward areas to remove regional imbalances. This paper analyses the trends in financing of SSIs by OSFC in the State particularly in the context of giving fill up to SSIs to face the challenge of competition in the years to come.

SSIs in India and Emerging Challenges

Recognising the importance of SSIs having high potentials for growth in output, employment, exports and wider dispersal of industrial bases using local skills and resources, the Govt. of India since the enunciation of the First Industrial Policy Resolution in 1948 have been providing necessary impetus through appropriate polices and institutional support to this sector. As per the latest available information the total number of SSIs units in India in 1998-99 stood at 31.21 lakh producing Rs. 5,27,515 Cr of output of which Rs. 49.481 Cr were exported.[3] The overall position of SSIs during the post-reform period is depicted in Table-2.1.

Table—2.1 Overal Performance of SSIs in India

Year	*No. of Units (in lakh)*	*Output at Current Price (Rs. in Cr.)*	*Employment (Lakh Nos.)*	*Export at Current Price (Rs. in Cr.)*
1991-92	20.82	1,78,699	129.80	13,883
1992-93	22.46	2,09,300	134.06	17,785
1993-94	23.81	2,41,648	139.38	25,307
1994-95	25.71	2,93,990	146.56	29,068
1995-96	27.24	3,56,213	152.61	36,470
1996-97	28.57	4,12,636	160.00	39,249
1997-98	30.14	4,65,171	167.20	44,437
1998-99 (P)	31.21	5,27,515	171.58 (p)	49,481

P =Provisional, P = Projected.

Govt. of India, Economic Survey 1999-2000, p. 126.

From an isolated and protective environment, the Indian economy since mid-eighties and more particularly from July 1991 is passing through perceptible liberalisation and transitional period of integrating itself with global economies. Besides at the global level, there is a significant technological revolution of world wide free trade and regional groupings are other notable developments of current times. All these events are making profound impact on the existence and growth of small enterprises which now have to face new challenges and opportunities. India, being a signatory to WTO agreement, its industries would no longer be able to avail the benefits of quantitative and tariff restrictions. All ready in the 2000-01 EXIM Policy, 714 items have been removed from quantitative restriction (QR) list and further 715 items are stated to go by March 2001[4]. Abid Hussain Committee in 1997 has recommended for the withdrawal of the prevailing benefits of reservation of items produced in SSI sector. In view of these developments, now SSIs are bound to face stiff competition from large scale domestic producers, multinational corporations (MNCs) and free imports from abroad. In this new environment, SSIs are required to overcome the redundancy in manufacturing technology, management techniques and marketing strategy to stay competitive in the market place. The strategy to promote the SSIs must be aligned to the general industrial growth strategy, globalisation thrusts and business revival plans of the large and the small.[5]

According to the information complied by RBI from commercial banks, there were 2,24,012 sick/weak units consisting of 2,21,536 units (98.89%) in the SSI sector and balance 2476 (1.11%) in the Non-SSI sector as on 31st March 1998. Out of the total Rs. 15,682 Cr. Bank credit blocked in sick industries nearly 24.6% were blocked in the SSI Sector.[6] Further studies reveal that the problems of timely credit (banks adopt security based approach rather than need based to advance credit), frequent changes in govt. policies relating to custom tariffs, excise duties, other taxes etc., and bureaucratic hurdles from State Tax and other inspecting agencies are primarily responsible for growing incidence of sickness in nearly 70% of sick units.[7]

SSIs in Orissa

The Govt. of Orissa from the very beginning has adopted the industrialisation programme through the promotion of SSIs to take care of poverty, unemployment and regional imbalances in the State. Following the Govt. of India's economic reforms, the reformulated Industrial Policy 1996 of the State aims at harnessing the potentials of vast natural resources consistent with the protection of environment for accelerated industrial growth. The new policy inter alias envisages the strengthening of rural economy through development of agro-based industries, small industries, village and cottage industries, sericulture, handloom and handicraft. Development of skills and more particularly the stimulation and broadening of entrepreneurial base constitute and integral part of the policy. In the new organisational set up, DIC will operate as nodal agency for the development of SSIs and for recommending grant of various incentives. The Govt. of Orissa have taken steps to establish DICs in all newly created 17 districts and district Collectors are authorised to allocate land upto 5 acres and to ensure supply of power, water etc. through co-ordination with different agencies. The overall small scale industrial scenario of the State can be visualised from Table-2.2.

Table—2.2 Position of SSIs in Orissa

Year	*No. of SSIs Set up*	*Investment at (Rs. in Cr.)*	*Employment (No. of person)*
Upto 1989-90 (by end of 7th Plan)	35,867	437.26	2,65,332
1990-91	2,249	61.00	15,657
1991-92	2,233	52.03	15,545
1992-93	2,117	55.00	13,344
1993-94	2,311	56.21	13,807
1994-95	2,327	68.08	13,096
1995-96	2,507	74.82	13,019
1996-97	3,098	104.53	15,629
1997-98	3,186	134.09	16,716
1998-99	3,184	190.06	16,776
Total	**59,079**	**1,233.08**	**3,98,921**

Source: Directorate of Industries, Orissa, Cuttack.

Finance: The Critical Input

The financial needs of SSIs are met by the entrepreneur themselves and also through institutional sources. While the term loan requirements are met by SFCs, the working capital needs are met by commercial banks. After banks nationalisation, the volume of credit to SSIs has been increasing steadily, as advances to this sector have been brought under priority lending category. The single window scheme (SWS) for financing fixed assets and working capital of tiny and SSI units was introduced in May 1988. The set up of the Small Industries Development Bank of India (SIDBI) in 1990 as an apex bank for priority sector refinancing through various schemes is another major policy initiative of the Govt. of India to meet the growing credit requirements of the sector. A nation-wide survey on the problems and prospects of SSI sector by FICCI reveals that the delay in the delivery of credit as fast as possible as delays cause problems like obsolescence, inability to stick to delivery schedule of items, cost overruns etc.[8] In place of Delayed Payment Act, majority of respondents prefer a scheme of discounting small firms receivables from large units, banks and financial institutions to ensure timely and adequate credit to the SSI sector.

Finance to SSIs by OSFC

OSFC provides long term finance to SSIs while refinance facility is available from IDBI and SIDBI. It has emerged as the largest long term financing institution and has remained primarily responsible for growth, expansion and dispersal of SSIs in the State. It also plays a vital role in developing SSIs in the backward districts for making frontal attack on poverty and regional inequalities.

Table-2.3 highlights the total financial assistance extended by OSFC in terms of sanctions and disbursements during 1987-88 till 1998-99. Sanctions to 12,218 units of Rs. 72,641,73 lakh and disbursement to 8,731 units amounting to Rs. 60,535,48 lakh were made during the study period of 12 years. The average amount sanctioned was Rs. 5.95 lakh per unit as against Rs. 6.93 lakh per unit of average disbursement during the same period. The disbursement/sanction ratio for the whole period came out to be 83.33 per cent. It is also evident from the table that after 1995-96, there has been decline in sanctions of the corporation due to East

Table—2.3 Total Sanction and Disbursement of Loans by O.S.F.C

(Amount in Rs.lakh)

Year	*Sanctions*		*Av. Amount sanctioned per unit*	*Disbursement*		*Av. Amount disbursed per unit*	*Disbursement/ Sanction ratio in percent*
	No. of units	*Amount*		*No. of units*	*Amount*		
1987-88	1227	4733.38	3.85	887	4904.91	5.52	103.62
1988-89	1794	6662.17	3.71	640	5869.60	9.17	88.10
1989-90	1527	5837.77	3.82	631	5611.91	8.89	96.13
1990-91	1167	4970.47	4.25	725	4969.49	6.85	99.98
1991-92	1042	4942.43	4.74	974	5078.42	5.21	102.75
1992-93	859	5515.58	6.42	796	4927.58	6.19	89.33
1993-94	973	5094.90	5.23	756	4586.06	6.06	90.01
1994-95	582	3885.85	6.67	558	3511.55	6.29	90.36
1995-96	1014	8440.09	8.32	873	5452.09	6.24	64.59
1996-97	936	8050.45	8.60	873	5452.09	6.24	67.72
1997-98	574	7700.56	13.42	545	5522.49	10.13	71.72
1998-99	523	6808.08	13.02	473	4649.29	9.83	68.30
Total	**12,218**	**72,641.73**	**5.95**	**8,731**	**60,535.48**	**6.93**	**83.33**
Cumulative since inception	**43,135**	**96,611.75**	**2.24**	**24,783**	**86,657.83**	**3.50**	**89.70**

Source: OSFC, Annual Reports, Cuttack, Orissa.

Asian Currency Crisis and consequent economic slowdown sets in the national economy. Since inception till 1998-99 the corporation has accorded sanctions in respect of 43,135 units with Rs. 96,611.75 lakh and disbursement of 24,783 units with Rs. 86,657.83 lakh giving rise to disbursement/sanction ratio of 89.70 per cent.

Table-2.4 reflects the trends in corporation's financial assistance to SSIs during 1987-88 to 1998-99. Sanctions were made in respect of total 4815 SSI units with Rs. 37081.17 lakh and disbursement for 2984 SSI units with Rs. 33,194,51 lakhs resulted in 89.52 per cent of disbursement/sanction ratio during these twelve years of study period, hotel, nursing home etc., SSIs account for major chunk of sanctions and disbursements. So far as sanction is concerned, SSIs share is 39.41 per cent of total units and 51.05 per cent of total sanctions. In disbursement front, the corresponding shares of SSI are 34.18 per cent in units and 54.83 per cent in amount while the average amount sanctioned per unit come out Rs. 7.64 lakh, the average amount of disbursement per unit stood at Rs. 11.12 lakh during the same period.

Table-2.5 reveals the purpose wise classification of sanctions viz., new projects, rehabilitation and expansion/modernisation made by OSFC to SSIs in the state. Throughout the study period, financing of new projects received top most priority followed by expansion and/or modernisation of existing units of the corporation. Both unit wise and amount-wise, rehabilitation programme received least attention for nurturing the weak and sick units. In the post-reform period the quantum of financial assistance to new units varied between 50.54 per cent in 1994-95 to highest of 89.47 per cent in 1995-96. In absolute terms, the year 1998-99 witnessed highest amount of financial flow i.e. Rs. 3723.11 lakh to new project.

Table-2.6 exhibits area-wise/district-wise break-up of financial assistance provided by OSFC basing on the degree of backwardness of the region during 1987-88 to 1996-97. Undivided 13 districts were classified into 3 groups viz. (a) No industry districts (b) Backward districts and (c) Other than Backward districts i.e. industrially advanced districts. In the no-industry districts, the volume of sanctions varied between the lowest of Rs. 87.84 lakh in

Table—2.5 Purpose-wise Classification of Sanctions (Effective) by O.S.F.C to SSIs

(Amount in Rs. lakh)

Year	New Projects		Rehabilitation		Expansion/Modernisation	
	No.	Amount in Rs. lakh	No.	Amount in Rs. lakh	No.	Amount in Rs. lakh
1	2	3	4	5	6	7
1987-88	N.A.	N.A.	N.A.	N.A.	N.A.	N.A.
1988-89	196 (37.91)	2046.62 (61.63)	40 (7.73)	238.82 (7.19)	281 (54.36)	1035.84 (31.18)
1989-90	197 (42.55)	1496.53 (58.27)	56 (12.10)	319.18 (12.43)	210 (45.35)	752.53 (29.30)
1990-91	191 (58.95)	1671.88 (72.31)	32 (9.87)	196.69 (8.50)	101 (31.18)	443.68 (19.19)
1991-92	150 (66.08)	1108.71 (70.76)	15 (6.60)	93.33 (5.96)	62 (27.32)	364.85 (23.28)
1992-93	145 (77.54)	1948.64 (88.14)	5 (2.67)	26.20 (1.20)	37 (19.79)	221.07 (10.06)
1993-94	140 (70.71)	1485.89 (78.80)	3 (1.52)	60.91 (3.23)	55 (27.77)	338.97 (17.97)
1994-95	86 (62.78)	806.83 (50.54)	3 (2.19)	72.39 (4.53)	48 (35.03)	717.05 (44.93)

(Table Contd...)

1	2	3	4	5	6	7
1995-96	126	2460.22	2	26.50	52	263.14
	(70.00)	(89.47)	(1.11)	(0.961)	(28.89)	(9.57)
1996-97	191	2638.83	5	30.00	25	535.53
	(86.43)	(82.38)	(2.26)	(0.941)	(11.31)	(16.71)
1997-98	318	3373.94	12	104.46	27	2119.67
	(89.01)	(60.27)	(3.36)	(1.87)	(7.56)	(37.86)
1998-99	224	3723.11	1	6.00	87	645.11
	(71.79	(85.11)	(0.33)	(0.14)	(27.88)	(14.75)

Figures in brackets indicate percentage of total.

Source: OSFC, Annual Reports, Cuttack, Orissa.

Table—2.6 Area-wise/District-wise (Broad Group) Analysis of Financial Assistance to SSIs

(Amount in Rs. lakh)

Year	No. Industry districts				Backward Districts				Other Districts			
	Sanctions		Disbursement		Sanctions		Disbursement		Sanctions		Disbursement	
	Amount	Av. Amt.	Amount	Av. Amt.	Amount	Av. Amt.	Amount	Av. Amt.	Amount	Av. Amt.	Amount	Av. Amt.
1987-88	691.36 (134)	5.15	636.35 (86)	7.39	392.29 (161)	2.43	376.89 (106)	3.55	2014.58 (459)	4.38	2046.32 (269)	7.60
1988-89	852.76 (129)	6.61	965.51 (60)	16.09	320.08 (155)	2.06	336.68 (47)	7.16	2607.59 (579)	4.50	2698.15 (183)	14.74
1989-90	718.49 (108)	6.65	1395 (60)	23.25	177.79 (85)	2.09	326.46 (47)	6.94	2171.72 (565)	3.84	2275.25 (133)	17.10
1990-91	456.94 (92)	4.96	624.53 (35)	17.84	328.08 (83)	3.95	295.41 (37)	7.98	1944.91 (281)	6.92	1731.04 (98)	17.66
1991-92	374.45 (77)	4.86	445.66 (69)	6.45	274.83 (48)	5.72	263.05 (62)	4.24	1334.27 (174)	7.66	1418.95 (127)	11.17
1992-93	371.82 (44)	8.45	387.41 (65)	5.96	239.15 (30)	7.97	205.70 (27)	7.61	2072.07 (178)	11.64	1572.68 (149)	10.55
1993-94	253.28 (32)	7.91	292.50 (23)	12.71	341.87 (38)	8.99	185.70 (20)	9.28	1519.26 (156)	9.73	2051.12 (155)	13.23
1994-95	87.84 (17)	5.16	260.31 (25)	10.41	372.68 (36)	10.35	225.72 (31)	7.28	1136.11 (84)	13.52	1408.84 (116)	12.14
1995-96	358.70 (18)	19.92	402.08 (22)	18.27	1075.37 (57)	18.86	696.87 (66)	10.55	1674.49 (123)	13.61	1355.74 (159)	8.52
1996-97	335.36 (21)	15.96	486.44 (30)	16.21	1241.23 (92)	13.49	115.88 (108)	10.70	1963.13 (129)	15.21	1980.5 (145)	13.65

Figures in Bracket indicate Number of SSI units.

Source: OSFC, Annual Reports, Cuttack, Orissa.

1994 and highest of Rs. 852.76 lakh in 1988-89. The comparative figures in backward-districts are Rs. 239.15 lakh in 1992-93 and Rs. 1,241.23 lakh in 1996-97 respectively, and in non-backward districts the corresponding figures were Rs. 1136.11 lakh in 1994-95 and highest of Rs. 2607.59 lakh in 1988-89. From the table, it is crystal clear that the quantum of financial assistance to no industry and backward districts was low compared to non-backward districts and flow of financial assistance was more in pre-reform period as compared to post-reform period. Hence OSFC should intensify its efforts in financing more number of SSI units in the no-industry and backward districts if it is genuinely committed to the goal of reduction of regional disparities in the State.

Changes in SFC's Act and Scope of Activities in Reform ERA

With a view to enabling SFCs to finance/undertake new industrial/business activities since the on-set of economic reforms, the definition of industrial concern under Sec. 2(c) of the SFCs Act 1951 has been reviewed to include activities like construction of commercial complexes, show rooms, setting up of vocational training centres for imparting technical knowledge to entrepreneurs to set up and run units efficiently and produce quality goods and establishment of departmental stores, shopping malls and tourist homes. With the changing pattern of financing industrial enterprises, SFCs are giving thrust to their investment activities and capital market related operations. In view of this they have also started offering facilities such as equipment leasing and have entered the field of consultancy, merchant banking, debenture trusteeship and capital related services.[9] Further the amendments to SFC Act, 1951 was passed in the monsoon session (2000-01) of the Parliament and was assented to by the president of India on Sept. 12, 2000. The Act is amended to enable SFCs to equip themselves to the new emerging environment. The following changes are made in the amended Act.[10]

(i) The Share Capital held by IDBI will be transferred to SIDBI. Hence, now SIDBI which have a major say in the functioning of SFCs;

(ii) The Board of directors of all SFCs stand dissolved. This would reduce the political interference by State governments in the corporations;

(iii) A whole lot of new industries now look forward to financial assistance from SFCs which include information technology (IT), medical services, tourism related facilities, road building and maintenance, floriculture, poultry farming etc.;

(iv) The loan sanctioning limit of the corporation has been enhanced to Rs. 5 Cr. against the current limit of 2.40 Cr.

On the basis of these above amendments a high level committee has been constituted under the chairmanship of Sri G.P. Gupta, the Chairman and MD of IDBI to recommend measures to restructure the corporations. On the whole, these amendments are targeted at restructuring the capital of SFCs to increase authorised capital, enlarge shareholders base, permit share capital upto 49 per cent to public and remove restriction on the sale of bonds, debentures and borrowing money by SFCs.

Conclusion

Realising the significance of SSIs economy of the nation, governments both at the centre and in the State of Orissa have been deliberately pursuing SSI- friendly policies since the pronouncement of the first Industrial Policy Resolution in 1948. Orissa State Financial Corporation (OSFC) being the provider of long-term finance to small and medium enterprises (SMEs) is entrusted with the tasks of diversification of industrial base, growth of entrepreneurship, reduction of regional inequalities, revival of industrial sickness etc. in the State. The analysis of aggregate sanctions and total disbursement reveals that during the study period i.e. 1987-88 to 1998-99, the corporation achieved the disbursement/sanction ratio of 83.33 per cent as against 89.70 per cent disbursement/sanction ratio since inception till March 1999. On the whole the performance of OSFC in sanction and disbursement front is considered superior when compared with disbursement sanction ratio of 81.87 per cent for all SFCs in the country. The foregoing analysis also reveals that SSIs are the major recipients of financial assistance from OSFC compared to other sectors as during the 12 years of study period. 51.01 per cent to total sanctions and 54.83 per cent of disbursements were made in respect of SSIs. The disbursement/sanction ratio of 89.52 per cent is also higher than national average which is 86.58 per cent. The analysis of purpose-wise classification of sanctions portrays that financing of new projects received major chunk of assistance, followed by expansion and modernisation of existing SSI units. However, it is disturbing to note that financial assistance to no-industry and backward districts taken together fell short of assistance provided to developed district during 1987-88 to 1996-97. Hence deliberate but concerted efforts are necessary on the part of the corporation to enhance the quantum of assistance to backward and no-industry districts as per with developed districts to remove regional imbalance. The new and reformulated industrial policies of the State in tandem with economic reforms program of the centre on the one hand and the latest amendments to SFC Act 1951 concerning dissolution of OSFC's boards for greater operational autonomy of corporations, enhancement of loan sanctioning limit to Rs. 5 Cr. from current limit of 2.40 Cr. Allowing new lots of industries like IT, medical services, road building and maintenance, floriculture etc. to avail financial assistance, restructuring capital, shareholder's base (49% of capital offered to public) etc. on the other would hopefully enable SSI to compete and grow in the new changing global environment.

REFERENCES

1. "Doing without Reservation in Small Sector", Editorial, *The Southern Economist*, Vol. 39, No. 10, Sept. 15, 2000, pp. 1-3.
2. Ibid.
3. Govt. of India, "*Small Scale Industry*", Economic Survey 1999-2000, Ministry of Finance, Economic Division, New Delhi, March 2000, p. 126.
4. State Bank Economic News Letter "*Exim Policy 2000-01 - Life after QR (Quantitative Restrictions) Vol. XXXIV*, No. 15 Mumbai, April 10, 2000, p. 59.
5. Mukerjee S.K., "Large, Medium & Small Firms All Coexist", ET interface,. *The Economic Times*, Vol. 40, No. 284, Calcutta, Sept. 20, 2000, p. 8.
6. Govt. of India, "*Industrial Sickness*" Economic Survey 2000-01, Ministry of Finance, Economic Division, New Delhi, March 2000, pp. 126-127.
7. Bhat T.P., Saxena V & Gupta H, "*Impact of WTO Agreement on Small & medium Enterprises (SMEs) in India, The Indian Journal of Commerce*, Vol. 53, No. 122, New Delhi, Jan-June 2000, p. 3.

8. Assocham "Better Credit for SSI Needed", Survey published in *The New Indian Express*, Bhubaneswar, Aug. 5, 1999, p. 15.

9. Industrial Development Bank of India (IDBI) "*State Financial Corporations*", Report on Development Banking in India (20th) 1998-99, Mumbai, pp. 77-80.

10. Kuber G, "Act Changes to See the Death of SFC Boards" *The Economic Times*, Calcutta, Oct. 5, 2000, p. 10.

3

Institutional Finance for Small Scale Sector

The Orissan Picture

Dr. Nisha Jain*

Dr. Sanjay Ku. Satapathy**

The small industries constitute a large share in the planned development of Indian Economy. It accounts for about 50 per cent of the industrial production in the country and 80 per cent of the employment in the industrial sector. This sector plays a crucial role in the process of economic development in general and industrial development in particular by value addition, employment generation, removing regional disparities, contribution to exports etc. About one-fourth of the exports is shared by these industries and considering the non-traditional items it is about 40 per cent. The small industries are not only important because of their numerical volume but also frequently justified from the grand that they are capital saving and can animate vast idle resources of labour and managerial talent.

* **Faculty Member, Department of Commerce, R.D. Women's College, Bhubaneswar.**

** **Faculty Member, Department of Commerce, R.D. Women's College, Bhubaneswar.**

Orissa Scenario

The state of Orissa came into being on 1st April 1948. The State comprising of 4.74% of India's land mass account for 3.74% of India's population. Located on the Maritime route connecting the European continent and the Asian countries. Orissa is the mineral store house of India accounting for nearly 98% of chrome ore, 95% of nickel, 70% of bauxite, 26.08% of iron ore and 24% of coal. The state also has goods reserves of precious and semi-precious stones, fertile soil, unique advantage of 480 km of coastal brackish and raverine ecosystem.

In the backdrop, the present paper attempts to find out the growth of SSI units in Orissa over a period of 10 years i.e. 1991-2001, the various sources of finance to SSI's and institutions, providing support to SSIs.

An industrial undertaking in which the investment in fixed assets in plant and machinery whether held on ownership firms or on lease or on hire purchase does not exceed Rs. 300 lakhs come within the purview of small scale industrial undertaking w.e.f. 10.12.97 (Notification No. 857 dated 10.12.97)

Growth of SSI Units

Table-3.1 shows the growth in the number of SSI units from 1990-91 to 1999-2000 and the growth rate.

Table—3.1 Growth of SSI Unit in Orissa

Year	*No. of SSI*	*Growth Rate*	*Share to all India (in %)*
1990-91	38094	6.3	2.0
1991-92	40327	5.9	1.9
1992-93	42444	5.4	1.9
1993-94	44755	5.4	1.9
1994-95	47082	5.2	1.8
1995-96	49589	5.3	1.8
1996-97	52687	6.2	1.8
1997-98	55873	6.0	1.9
1998-99	59057	5.6	1.9
1999-2000	62530	5.3	–

Source: Directorate of Industries, Orissa & SIDO.

Table-3.2 presents the growth of investment and employment per SSI units, over the time. It shows that employment per SSI unit has declined but investment had been increasing over the years indicating that SSI sector has become more capital intensive over the period.

Table—3.2 Investment and employment per SSI units in Orissa

(Rs. in lakhs)

Item/Year	*1980-81*	*1990-91*	*1994-95*	*1997-98*	*1998-99*	*1999-2000*
Employment (No) per SSI Unit	8.08	7.37	7.14	4.97	4.97	5.06
Investment per SSI unit	0.73	1.30	1.54	2.88	3.84	4.03
Investment per units of employment	0.09	0.17	0.21	0.58	0.77	0.80

Source: Orissa State Profile, SISI, Cuttack.

The growth of SSIs have not contributed much in rectifying the regional imbalance within the state as its growth continue to remain concentrated in the so-called advanced districts. Although a host of incentives and subsidies are provided to start industrial units in the backward districts. This could not lure the investors because of the lack of infrastructural facilities. The district wise no. of SSI units set up, with investment and employment during 1999-2000 is reflected in Table-3.3.

Table—3.3 District wise No Investment and Employment of SSI units set up during 1999-2k

Sl. No.	*Name of the District*	*No.*	*Investment (Rs. in lakhs)*	*Employment*
1	2	3	4	5
1.	Angul	122	275.29	407
2.	Balasore	205	1345.81	1378
3.	Baragarh	115	790.91	684
4.	Bhadrak	92	317.02	425
5.	Bolangir	102	281.17	392
6.	Boudh	26	27.07	90
7.	Cuttack	268	1780.60	1722

(Table Contd...)

1	2	3	4	5
8.	Deogarh	15	13.56	547
9.	Dhenkanal	85	110.05	384
10.	Gajapati	62	115.90	336
11.	Ganjam	234	1762.56	1517
12.	Jagatsinghpur	90	167.87	362
13.	Jajpur	285	222.39	583
14.	Jharsugada	61	209.37	334
15.	Kalahandi	60	255.15	246
16.	Kandhamal	56	70.40	202
17.	Kendrapara	74	84.49	318
18.	Keonjhar	118	1125.63	719
19.	Khurda	253	2030.97	1625
20.	Koraput	113	647.59	904
21.	Malkangiri	30	215.26	181
22.	Mayurbhanj	198	539.03	864
23.	Nawarangpur	56	377.50	302
24.	Nayagarh	56	77.46	305
25.	Nuapada	29	55.72	137
26.	Puri	114	556.36	721
27.	Rayagada	105	392.96	609
28.	Sambalpur	88	315.93	285
29.	Sonepur	53	62.29	264
30.	Sundargarh	408	1967.51	2258
	Total	**3473**	**16293.82**	**18608**

Source: Directorate of Industries, Cuttack

Source of Finance

Credit is the main input for sustained growth of the small scale sector and its availability continues to be a matter of concern.

The small- scale industrial sector is provided working capital by commercial banks and in some cases by cooperative banks and regional rural banks. Term loans are provided by State Financial Corporations (SFCs). Small Industries Development Corporation (SIDCs) National Small Industries Corporation (NSIC) and National Bank of Agriculture and Rural Development (NABARD) small sized

SSI and tiny units also get some term loans from commercial banks along with working capital in the form of composite loans.

Reference to these institution is provided by the Small Industries Development Bank of India (SIDBI). Such reference comprises assistance provided to State Financial Corporation Bills, Finance scheme, Seed Capital Scheme new debt instrument and to NSIC. Long term loans are provided to the SSI units by SFCs mainly through single window scheme and National Equity Fund some part of working capital for pre-operative expenses is also provided by SFCs to small-scale industrial unit under the single window scheme.

Institutional Support

For the promotion and development of SSIs many Governmental Agencies both by the central as well as state have been set up to provide institutional support. The following discussion will be under two major heads.

A. CENTRAL GOVERNMENT ORGANISATIONS/AGENCIES

B. ORGANISATIONS UNDER STATE GOVERNMENT

A. Central Government Organisations/Agencies

The various organisations / agencies set up under the Central Govt. and their functions in Orissa is being discussed:

1. National Small Industries Corporation (NSIC)

The NSIC was set up by the Government of India for promotion and development of SSI in the country by way of supplying machineries on hire purchase scheme, material, marketing assistance etc. The NSIC local branch in Orissa has a common facility centre located at Khapuria Industrial Estate, Cuttack to provide testing and laboratory facilities to various SSIs. It provides support to small scale sector in the following areas :

- Supply of indigenous and imported machines on easy line purchase terms.
- Procurement and supply of indigenous and imported raw materials.

- Single point registration scheme.
- Supply of both indigenous and imported machines on lease basis to existing units for expansion, diversification and modernisation.
- Marketing and Exports of Products.

2. Khadi and Village Industries Commission (KVIC)

The main objectives of the commission is to develop Khadi and Village Industries for generating more employment opportunities in the rural areas.

The commissions' functions are to give financial as well as technical assistance to the Khadi & Village Industries throughout the country. The KVIC State office is located at Bhubaneswar.

3. National Productivity Council (NPC)

The NPC is an undertaking of Ministry of Industry, Govt. of India and it provides training, consultancy and technical services to industries and organisation in the country.

The organisation seeks alliance to provide training and consultancy in the areas of restructuring sectorial study in industry and agriculture, productivity norms, productivity measurement and monitoring, wage administration, materials management, operation research, ISO-9000 series certification and many other such operation.

4. Bureau of Indian Standards (BIS)

The BIS has been functioning under the Ministry of Civil Supplies Consumer Affairs and Public Distributor, Government of India. The functions of BIS are as follows:

- Establishment, publication and promotion and adoption of Indian standard.
- Inspection of articles or process under certification scheme.
- Promotion of standardisation and its development.
- Recognising quality assurance system in manufacturing and processing units.

- Formulation, implementation and coordination of activities relating to quality maintenance and improvements in products and processes.

5. Small Industries Service Institute (SISI)

Small Industries Service Institute (SISI), Cuttack, a field office of Small Industries Development Organisation under the Ministry of Industry and ARI, Government of India. The primary aim of this institute is to promote and develop small scale industries in the state of Orissa by rendering various services. Some of the important activities of this institute are

- To conduct District Industrial Potentiality Survey.
- To render techno economic and managerial consultancy.
- To provide training facilities under Entrepreneurship Development Programme (EDP) and Management Development Programme (MDP).
- To provide assistance/consultancy to prospective entrepreneur.
- To provide export related assistance.
- Revival of sick SSI units.
- To conduct worship, seminars and awareness programme.

6. Central Tool Room and Training Centre (CTTC)

The CTTC, Bhubaneswar run as a government of India society under SIDO is a Indo-Danish Tool Room Project. It performs the following functions:

- Assistance to develop new tool design.
- Manufacture of tools, fixtures, moulds etc.
- Consultancy
- Technical training on short term and long term basis.

7. Minerals and Metal Trading Corporation Ltd. (MMTC)

MMTC is engaged in the export of Iron Ore, Chrome Ore, Marine products, Leather products, Textiles, Gems and Jewelleries etc. It imports product like NF metals, fertilisers, gold palmolein. It is also involved in domestic trading of oil and oil seeds, pulses, turmeric sal wood etc. The organisation offers services such as business link, finance marketing research and development.

MMTC Ltd., Bhubaneswar is engaged in setting up Steel Plants and parts in the state. The company is financing the Gopalpur port for converting it into an all weather prot in alliance with TISCO and the state govt.

8. Export Credit Guarantee Corporation of India Ltd. (ECGC)

The organisation, a government of India undertaking supports and strengthens the export promotion drive in the country by providing a range of credit risk insurance covers to exporters against loss in export of goods and services. It also offers guarantees to banks and financial institutions to enable exporters, obtain better facilities from them. The main offers issued by ECGC are:

- Standard policy issued to exporter to protect them against payment risk involved in exports on short term credit and small export policy issued to exporter with small export.
- Financial guarantees issued to banks in India to protect them from risk of loss involved in their extending financial support to exporter.
- Special schemes viz. transfer guarantee, exchange fluctuation risk insurance, overseas investment insurance and others.

9. Industrial Development Bank of India (IDBI)

The main objective of IDBI is to extend financial assistance for setting up large and medium scale industrial units in the country.

10. Industrial Finance Corporation of India Ltd. (IFCI)

The main objective of the IFCI is to provide medium and long term credit for readily available to industrial concerns in India. The major functions of the IFCI is term lending merchant bankers, Financial services etc. The state office of IFCI is located at Bhubaneswar.

11. Small Industries Development Bank of India (SIDBI)

This principal financial institutions for promotion financing and development of the small-scale sector. The organisation provides following:

- Provides terms loans to SSI units for financial new expansion diversification and modernisation of existing projects.
- Provides terms loans to marketed agencies for developing marketing outlets for SSI product.
- Providing term loans to leasing and HP companies for offering leasing and hire purchase facilities to SSI units.
- Foreign currency loan for import of equipment by existing export oriented SSIs.
- Provide equity type soft loans to:
  - — Women entrepreneurs to set up new units under Mahila Udyog Nidhi Scheme.
  - — New Project/existing units for expansion/diversification potentially viable sick units and service enterprises under the National Equity Fund Scheme.
- Provides Refinance
  - — Loans for financing fixed asset as well as worker's capital through the same agencies viz. state level Institution or bank under single windows.
  - — Loans granted by banks and state level institutions for new SSI projects and for expansion, modernisation quality promotion, diversification and rehabilitation.
- Provides bills finance for direct discounting of medium term, usance bills short term bills rediscounting of long term usance bills and short term bills.
- Provides Venture Capital for small scale entrepreneurs using innovative indigenous technology and expertise.

The state office of SIDBI is located in Bhubaneswar.

B. Some Organisations Under State Governments

1. Directorate of Industries, Orissa

This is an apex organisation of the State Government under the Dept. of Industries which looks after the entire promotional activities relating to small scale and other cottage industries including medium as well as large scale industries. It also overseas the work of the District Industries Centre.

2. District Industries Centre

These centres are situated in all the districts headquarters of the state as the field office of Directorate of Industries. The function of DIC relates providing registered of SSI units, preparation of schemes, feasibility report, arrangement of land, scarce raw materials marketing assistance training and etc.

3. Orissa State Finance Corporation (OSFC)

The OSFC provides financial services like term loans for settings up small and medium scale industries acquisition of transport vehicles and settings up of hotels, nursing home, clinic etc. It also plays a crucial role in rehabilitation of sick SSI limits in the state.

4. Orissa Small Industries Corporation (OSIC)

This corporation is entrusted to deal with scarce raw materials viz. Iron and Steel, Pig Iron, CI melting scrap, Paraffin wax, Plastic material, Newsprint etc. to SSI units in Orissa. It has been registered as an export house. It receives enquires and orders from overseas buyers disseminate the orders among the competent and capable SSI units of the state. Later, it collects the finished goods from them and exports the items.

Besides this the organisation also undertakes preparation of project reports conducting feasibility studies, providing project consultancy services revival of sick unit in small scale sector and etc.

5. Institute of Entrepreneurship Development

This institute provides training, counselling and consultancy services to small and medium entrepreneurs.

It is a nodal agency in the field of entrepreneur development in the state. It has trained more than 650 entrepreneurs to set up small scale industries in the state. The organisation seeks alliance with university and institute in the areas of farming panel to enrol the faculty members for interaction, planning and finalising course curriculum and other programmes relevance to the development of entrepreneurs.

6. Industrial Promotion and Investment Corporation of Orissa Ltd. (IPICOL)

IPICOL is an establishment of government of Orissa undertaking in Bhubaneswar. Its objective is to accelerate the individual development activity in the state by inviting investors to invest in large and medium scale industries. The various services provided are:

- Identification of viable industrial projects
- Identification of Ideal Entrepreneurs to implement such projects
- Provide finance for industrial project
- Co-ordination with Govt. for providing basic amenities such as power, land, water and raw material
- Operating the refinancing scheme of IDBI and SIDBI and others.

7. Directorate of Export Promotion and Marketing

Directorate of Export Promotion and Marketing is the nodal agency for issue of detailed guidelines for implementation of export promotion and market support facilities extended to local industries. The principal objectives of this organisation are:

- To provide marketing assistance to SSI units of the state.
- To promote exports from the state.

Conclusion

Orissa is endowed with vast natural and human resources which can be used for industrial development. Despite, its vast resources, it continues to be one of the industrial backward states of the country.

In spite of the varied institutions to provide finance and other services, it has been observed that the inability to provide adequate security to banks and low recovery are the major constraints in the flow of investment credit to SSI units. Moreover there is a dearth of technically sound and skilled entrepreneurs adequate infrastructure facilities in different areas in the state. If adequate attention is diverted in the area mentioned above, Orissa can excel in the small scale industries sector.

REFERENCES

1. Orissa State Profile, SISI, March 2001.
2. Small Scale Sector, Dept. of SSI, A & RI, January 1999.
3. *Economic Survey*, Govt. of Orissa, Bureau of Economics & Statistics, Bhubaneswar - 2000 - 2001.
4. Directorate of Industries, Orissa.
5. Ram K.V. *Modern Small Industry in India, Problems and Prospects*, Saga Publication, New Delhi.
6. Hoselitz, B.F. "Economic Growth and Rural Industrialisation", *Economic Weakly*, 001- 1958, pp. 291-302.

4

The Role of OSFC in the Development of SSIs in Response to Policy of Liberalisation of the Govt. of India in 1991-92

Sambit Mishra*

The state of national economy prior to 1991 showed a grim picture with the inflation rate rising to 17% in August, 1991 and a grave balance of payment position showing current account deficit of nearly 3% of the G.D.P. This forced the Govt. of India to adopt the policy of liberalization in 1991-92. This policy formulated by the Central Govt. forced the state Govt. to take some measures for the rapid industrial development. The Govt. of Orissa announced the new industrial policy in 1992. The industrial policy resolution of 1992 contained various incentives and concession for promotion of industries in Orissa. It was expected that the policy would lead to the achievement of the objective of major handicap in the industrial development. The enterprises always lack the financial resources to set up the large scale and medium scale industries. The only way to contribute to the national as well as the state economy is through the development of small scale industries. So the Govt. of Orissa gave priority to the development of small scale industries. In this contest the O.S.F.C. which a prominent financial institution in form

***Lecturer in Commerce, Kendrapara College.**

of public or statutory corporation of the state had a major role to play in financing the SSIs.

Objective of the Study

The objective of this study is to analyse the following:

(a) The extent of credit deployment by the O.S.F.C. in the development of SSI's in the state after the policy of liberalisation by the Govt. of India.

(b) The role played by it in the achievement of balanced industrial development of the regions through the industrial development of backward areas.

The deployment of credit by the O.S.F.C. in the development of SSIs in the state after the policy of liberalisation by the Govt. of India.

The O.S.F.C. is the Govt. financial agency in the form of public or statutory corporation. So it is expected that the policy of the Govt. would be implemented through its activities. The managing director of the O.S.F.C. had expressed in its annual report of 1992-93 that the liberalisation policy of the Govt. of India will be implemented through the deployment of credit for rapid industrialisation. But it is revealed from its performance as stated in Table-4.1 that the O.S.F.C. has not been able to achieve the desired objective. As on 31.3.92, the loan disbursed by the corporation to the small scale industries stood at Rs. 30610.71 lakhs amounting to 59.67% of the total loan disbursed by it. Out of this the loan disbursed to the tiny sector was Rs. 703.21 lakhs amounting to only 1.37% of the total loans and loan disbursed to other SSIs was Rs. 29907.5 lakhs amounting to 58.30% of total loan (as stated in Table-4.1) as on 31.3.96, the loan disbursed by the corporation to the SSIs stood at Rs. 39253.42 lakhs amounting to 56.25% of the total loan disbursed. Out of this the loan disbursed to the tiny sector was Rs. 889.4 lakhs amounting to only 1.27% of the total loan and the land disbursed to other SSIs was Rs. 38364.02 lakhs amounting to 54.98% of the total loans. The compound growth rate of the loan disbursed to the SSI's was only .064% from 31.3.92 to 31.3.96 the compound growth rate of loan disbursed to the tiny sector was .06% and other SSI units was .064% during this period. This was far from satisfactory.

Table—4.1 Sector-wise Deployment of Credit by the O.S.F.C.

Sl. No.	Sector	*As on 31.03.92 (Cumulative figure of disbursements)*				*As on 31.03.96 (Cumulative figure of disbursements)*				*As on 31.03.96 (Cumulative figure of disbursements)*			
		No.	*Amount in lakh of Rs.*	*%*	*Compound Growth rate*	*No.*	*Amount in lakh of Rs.*	*%*	*Compound Growth rate*	*No.*	*Amount in lakh of Rs.*	*%*	*Compound Growth rate*
1.	Small Scale Sector	12888	30610.71	59.67		13724	39253.42	56.25	.064%	14871	51215.71	55.48	0.68%
	a. Tiny Sector	6498	307.21	1.37		6585	889.40	1.27	.06%	6680	1444.82	1.57	.129%
	b. Other SSI Units	6390	29907.5	58.30		7139	38364.02	54.95	.064%	8191	49770.89	53.91	.067%
2.	Other Sectors	6917	20687.5	40.33		9064	30522.07	43.75	.10%	10568	41095.92	44.52	.077%
Total		**19805**	**51298.21**	**100**			**22788**	**69775.49**			**25439**	**92311.63**	

Source: Annual Report of O.S.F.C. for 1991-92, 1995-96 and 1999-2000.

The Compound Growth rate has been calculated through the following formula:

$Y_t = Y_0 (1 + r)^n$ Where, Y_t = Amount at the end of period

Y_0 = Amount in the beginning of the period

n = Number of the years in the period and

r = Compound growth rate

As on 31.3.2000 the loan disbursed by the corporation by the SSIs was Rs. 51215.71 lakhs amounting to 55.48% of the total loan disbursed by it. Out of this loan disbursed to tiny sector was Rs. 1444.82 lakhs amounting to 1.57% of the total loan disbursed and loan disbursed to other SSIs was Rs. 49770.89 lakhs amounting to 53.91% of the total loan disbursed. The compound growth rate of loan disbursed to the SSI's was only .068% from 31.3.96 to 31.3.2000. The compound growth rate of loan disbursed to the tiny sector was .129% and other SSI unit was .067% during this period. So the compound growth also fell below expectation during this period.

Role played by the O.S.F.C. in the achievement of balanced industrial development of the regions.

Balanced industrial development of all the regions is essential for the economic development of the nation. For removing the disparity in development of industries the districts of Orissa were classified into 3 categories known as

(a) No industry districts.

(b) Backward districts.

(c) Other districts. (Developed districts)

The object of the state Govt. was to develop more and more industries in the no industries districts and backward districts and the O.S.F.C. was expected to provide more loan to set up industries in those districts. But it can be seen from the data given in Table-4.2 that this objective has not been achieved by O.S.F.C.

Table-4.2 reveals that the amount of loan disbursed to the industries districts of un-divided Balasore, Bolangir and Phulbani in aggregate as on 31.3.92 since inception was Rs. 6055 lakhs which was only 19.78% of the total loan disbursed by the O.S.F.C. The loan disbursed to backward districts of undivided Dhenkanal, Keonjhar, Kalahandi, Koraput, Mayurbhanj in aggregate was Rs. 3893.56 lakhs as on 31.3.92 since inception which amount to only 12.72% of the total loan disbursed whereas the loan disbursed to the developed district like undivided Cuttack, Puri, Ganjan, Sambalpur and Sundargarh as on 31.3.92 since inception was Rs. 20662.15 lakhs which amount to 67.5% of the total loan disbursed. This shows remarkable disparity in the industrialization.

Table—4.2 District-wise Deployment of Credit by O.S.F.C. for SSI's

Districts	*As on 31.03.92*			*As on 31.03.92*			*As on 31.03.92*		
	No.	*Amount in lakh of Rs.*	*% of total*	*No.*	*Amount in lakh of Rs.*	*% of total*	*No.*	*Amount in lakh of Rs.*	*% of total*
Category A									
No Industry District (undivided)									
1. Balasore	738	4313.53		796	6347.07		872	6182.78	
2. Bolangir	578	1275.31		624	1508.52		668	1928.59	
3. Phulbani	191	466.16		222	541.71		241	634.71	
Total of category A	1507	6055.00	19.78	1642	7397.30	18.84	1781	8746.08	17.08
Category B									
Backward District (undivided)									
1. Dhenkanala	869	1164.68		891	1246.95		922	1612.46	
2. Keonjhar	269	375.18		273	415.61		298	858.06	
3. Kalahandi	290	520.74		307	663.07		342	1050.68	
4. Koraput	629	835.41		669	1185.07		791	2107.39	
5. Mayurbhanj	752	997.55		791	1295.15		838	1953.08	
Total of category B	2809	3893.56	12.72	2931	4805.49	12.24	3191	7581.67	14.80

(Table Contd...)

Category C									
Other District (undivided)									
1. Cuttack	4156	8197.33		4283	9720.84		4477	11389.25	
2. Puri	2908	7100.19		3071	9133.77		3247	11823.64	
3. Ganjam	538	1470.60		625	1908.51		752	2644.33	
4. Sambalpur	396	1120.72		473	2010.09		576	2935.91	
5. Sundergarh	574	2773.31		699	4277.42		847	6094.83	
Total of Category C	8572	20662.15	67.50	9151	27050.63	68.92	9899	34887.96	68.12
Total (A + B + C)	**12888**	**30610.71**	**100**	**13724**	**39253.42**	**100**	**14871**	**51215.71**	**100**

Despite the policy of minimizing the disparity there was no change in the disparity from 31.3.92 to 31.3.96. The loan disbursed to the no-industry districts as mentioned. Above as on 31.3.96 since inception was Rs. 7397.30 lakhs in aggregate amounting to only 18.84% of the total loan and to the backward districts Rs. 4805.49 lakhs in aggregate amounting to only 12.24% whereas to developed districts Rs. 27050.63 lakhs in aggregate since inception amounting to 68.92%.

There was no improvement in the situation even in the following years from 31.3.96 to 31.3.2000. The loan disbursed to no industry districts upto 31.3.2000 was Rs. 8746.08 amount to 17.08% of the total. The loan disbursed to the backward districts up to 31.3.2000 was Rs. 7581.67 lakhs amounting to 14.8% of the total whereas the loan disbursed to developed upto 31.3.2000 was Rs. 34887.96 lakhs amounting to 68.12% of the total.

It is evident from the above analysis that there is no change in the pattern of flow of assistance towards the industrially backward districts and no industry districts of the state by the O.S.F.C. despite the industrial policy of the backward development as lauded by the state Govt.

The following conclusion can be drawn from the study.

(a) That the O.S.F.C. has not responded favourably to the policy of liberalisation adopted by Govt. of India and there has been insignificant growth in the extent of finance provided by the corporation for the development of small scale industries. More efforts are needed in this regard.

(b) That the balanced industrial development of all the districts has not been achieved yet. More efforts are required to be taken by the O.S.F.C. for financing for the development of small scale industries in the districts.

(c) There is a need for encouragement and development of entrepreneurship in the state particularly in backward districts through concerted effort. The O.S.F.C. should focus its attention towards the development of No-industry and Backward districts so that the disparities in development can be minimized if not totally abolished.

5

Role of OSFC in the Development of Small Scale Industrial Sector

Mr. Deepak Kumar Mohanty*

Mr. Bana B. Mohanty**

A Critical Evaluation

Increasing pressure of the fast growing population, large and growing unemployment and consequent mass poverty are the major problems with which Indian planners have been grappling for the last five decades. The pace of economic growth has, however, not been adequate enough to alleviate the problems of rural and urban poor. The Sixth Five Year Plan has rightly focussed the attention on removal of unemployment and achieving an appreciable rise in the standard of living of the poorer sections of the population. Various measurers are being taken to increase the opportunities of gainful employment to masses and raise the productivity of agriculture and other rural pursuits through improved techniques, setting to suitable adequate credit facilities. The basic objective of planning activities with full sense of human dignity. The financial institutions, through its widening network of branches, is emerging as active partner in this endeavour. In any programme of increasing the volume of employment and increasing productivity, availability of

* Department of Commerce, Salipur College, Salipur.

** Department of Commerce, Salipur College, Salipur.

credit is of crucial importance. The financial institutions have thus been accorded a very important role in the development process of the country.

Economics Scenario of the State

After fifty years of planning and development, Orissa continues to remain one of the economically backward with a high incidence of poverty, in spite of the fact that it is endowed with fertile land abundant of water, rich mineral deposits, forest resources and human resources. The paradox of poverty is nowhere so remarkably visible as in the case of Orissa. This has been largely due to slow pace of industrial development. High dependence on and low productivity of the primary sector have resulted in significant fluctuations in the growth rate from year to year.

The state income and the per capita income which constitute the most dependable composite indicators of relative prosperity or backwardness of different states show that Orissa is one of the states having low or per capita income and the gap between National per capita and the state per capita had increased. During 1998-99, the state per capita income at constant (1993-94) prices was Rs. 5264 and at current prices Rs. 8435, as compared to National per capita income during the same period was Rs. 9739 at constant (1993-94) prices and Rs. 14,682 at current prices. The difference between the per capita income of the State and National levels for 1997-98 stood at Rs. 4283 at 1993-94 prices. The devastation caused by serve cyclone that hit Orissa in October 1999 will make it difficult to bridge this gap in the near future unless substantial resources from outside are made available. To reduce the disparity or to make people economically viable, industry is the only alternative engagement by which is growing unemployment problem can be solved.

The new Industrial Policy 1996, formulated in the context of the ongoing economic liberalisation reflects the State Government's commitment to growth and development of industries. The objectives of the new Industrial policy are to exploit the available natural to accelerate industrial growth with protection of environment, provide linkage between agriculture and agro and food processing industries, attract investment from outside, generate employment opportunities through industries like small scale industries, village and cotton industries, sericulture, handloom and handicrafts and strengthen and upgrade entrepreneurial skills.

The new Industrial Policy 1996, formulated in the context of the ongoing economic liberalisation reflects the State Government's commitment to growth and development of industries. The objectives of the new Industrial Policy are to exploit the available natural resources to accelerate industrial growth with protection of environment, provide linkage between agriculture and agro and food processing industries, attract investment from outside, generate employment opportunities through industries like small scale industries, village and cotton industries, sericulture, handloom and handicrafts and strengthen and upgrade entrepreneurial skills.

Frequent occurrence of natural calamities like drought, flood and cyclone stand as a barrier to economic progress of the state. The recent cyclones in the coastal districts of state have pushed the economy of the state bank by many years with consequential adverse impact on the development of the state.

Importance and Growth of Small Scale Sector

A significance feature of the Indian economy since independence is the rapid growth of the small industry sector. In the Industrial Policy Resolution 1948 and 1956, the small scale sector was given special role for creating additional employment with low capital investment. Industrial Policy Resolution 1956 stated that the small scale industries provide large scale employment, offer a method of ensuring a more equitable distribution of national income and facilities effective mobilisation of resources, remove regional disparities, remove economic imbalances and can produce goods and commodities for making them available at cheaper rates to meet the growing needs of rural India. A new thrust was given in favour of small units by Industrial Policy Statement of 1977.

The small scale enterprises were defined in 1966 as undertakings with a fixed capital investment of less than Rs. 7.5 lakhs and ancillaries with a fixed capital investment of Rs. 10 lakhs. In 1975, this limit was revised to Rs. 10 lakhs for small scale enterprises and Rs. 20 lakhs in case of ancillaries. Subsequently, under the industrial policy statement of 1980, this limit was further raised to Rs. 20 lakhs in case of small scale units and Rs. 25 lakhs in case of ancillaries. In March 1985, the Government has again revised the investment limit of small scale to Rs. 35 lakhs and for ancillary units to Rs. 45 lakhs. Under Industrial Policy statement of 1990, the investment limit has been raised from Rs. 35 lakhs to Rs. 60 lakhs and correspondingly for ancillaries from Rs. 45 lakhs to Rs. 75 lakhs. On the recommendation of Abid Hussain Committee, the Government has reduced fixed capital investment limit from Rs. 3 crores to Rs. 1 crore.

The small scale industrial sector which plays pivotal role in the Indian economy in terms of employment and growth, has recorded a high rate of growth since Independence in spite of stiff competition from the large scale sector and not so encouraging support from the Government. This is evidenced by the number of registered units which went up from 16,000 in 1950 to 36,000 units in 1961 and 4.2 lakhs in 1973-74 to 32.25 lakh units in 1999-2000. During the period from 1973-74 to 1999-2000, employment has grown from 4 million and output has increased from Rs. 7,200 crores to Rs. 5,78,470 crores. The average annual growth rate of employment in the small scale sector for the period 1980-81 to 1990-91 works out to be 5.8 per cent and that of production to be 18.6 per cent.

In Orissa, the number of SSI units established during 1999-2000 was 3473 having a total capital investment of Rs. 162.94 crores, generating employment to the tune of 18,608. The growth of SSI sector in Orissa can be evidenced from the table given below:

Table—5.1 Growth of Small Scale Industries in Orissa

Year	*No of SSI units established*	*Total capital investment (Rs. Crore)*	*Employment generated*
1996-97	3098	104.53	15629
1997-98	3186 (2.8)	134.09 (29.12)	16716 (6.96)
1998-99	3184 (-0.06)	190.06 (34.28)	16,776 (0.36)
1999-00	3473 (9.08)	162.94 (-14.27)	18608 (10.92)

Source: "Economic Survey 1999-00 and 2000-01" published by Govt. of Orissa.

Note: Figures in the brackets relate to growth rate (%) over the previous year.

From the above table, it is seen that though there is positive growth in terms of no of units and employment generation during 1999-2000, the total capital investment in SSI sector is showing a negative growth during the same period. The growth of capital investment in SSI is the highest at 34.28 per cent during 1998-99 within the last five years.

OSFC—A Brief History

It is generally agreed that while finance is not the only bottleneck in accelerating industrial growth rate in our economy, its availability in required quantum, form and on reasonable terms does constitute a significant factor in promoting industrial development. The Indian Industrial Commission recommended for the establishment of a specialised financial institution for industries, as early as in 1918. But the need for such an institution for industries was felt more seriously only during the post-World War II period and it was translated in to reality only after Independence. In fact, the year 1948 may be taken as the beginning of an era in providing industrial finance through the specialised institutions. As a follow up measure, the Industrial Finance Corporation of India (IFCI) was constituted on 1st July, 1948 under an Act of Parliament with a view to provide medium and long term credit to public limited companies and co-operative societies in the country. The small scale industries were kept outside the scope of IFCI. Ultimately, therefore, the State Financial Corporation (SFCs) Act was passed in the Parliament on 28th September, 1951 and the Act came in to force from Aug.1, 1952 with a view to meeting the deficiencies created by IFCI and commercial banks. The Act empowers the various State Governments to establish financial corporations in their respective states. Thus, OSFC was established in 1956 under the SFCs, Act, 1951, with the main object of providing institutional credit, both medium and long term, to the small and medium scale industrial concerns for construction of factory building, purchase of plant and machinery and renovation and modernisation of existing plant and machinery.

With a fast growth of industrialisation, the proportion of external goes on increasing to make the state industrially developed, OSFC whose operation covers the entire state, has been assigned a crucial role to play for the rapid industrialisation of the state by giving medium and long term financial assistance to small and medium sized industries.

PERFORMANCE OF OSFC

Overall Growth of Assistance

The overall growth of assistance by OSFC for the last five years can be well illustrated by the table-5.2 given below:

Table—5.2 Growth of Assistance Sanctioned (GROSS) to SSI Sector

Year	*Total assistance*	*Growth rate (%) Sector*	*Assistance to SSI*	*Growth Rate (%)*	*Share of SSI to total assistance (%)*
1995-96	84.40	–	27.50	–	32.58
1996-97	80.50	(-) 4.62	32.04	16.51	39.80
1997-98	77.00	(-) 4.35	55.98	74.72	72.70
1998-99	68.08	(-) 11.58	73.74	(-) 21.86	64.25
1999-00	106.70	56.73	72.15	64.95	67.62
Cumulative upto end March 2000	1228.87		694.41		56.51

Source: Annual Reports of OSFC.

From the above table, it is evident that though there were negative growth in total assistance sanctioned by OSFC in the year 1996-97 and 1997-98 the sanctions to SSI sector showed positive growth during the same periods. The year 1997-98 witnessed the highest share of SSI sector in the total assistance sanctioned. The share of SSI sector in the total assistance sanctioned upto end March 2000 is 56.51%.

Sector-wise Assistance

Sector-wise assistance by OSFC is reflected in the table-5.3 given below:

Table—5.3 Sector-wise Assistance Sanctioned to SSI Sector

Sl. No.	*Sector*	*1995-96*	*1996-97*	*1997-98*	*1998-99*	*1999-00*	*Cumulative up to end March 2000*
1.	Artisan/Village & Cottage Industries	0.01	–	–	–	5.61	11.07
2.	Tiny Sector	0.34	1.67	–	0.96	3.10	15.14
3.	Others	27.15	30.37	55.98	42.78	63.44	549.92
	Total	**27.50**	**32.04**	**55.98**	**43.74**	**72.15**	**576.13**

Source: Annual Reports of OSFC.

From the above table, it is evident that Artisan/village and Cottage industries registered that lowest share of assistance upto end-March 2000. During the period from 1996-97 to 1998-99 there was no sanction made to this sector. But in 1999-2000 sanctions were made to the tune of Rs. 5.61 crores to this sector. There was positive growth in the sanction made to Tiny sector during 1996-97 and 1999-2000, whereas negative growths were registered during 1996-97, 1997-98, 1998-99. The share of other sectors in the cumulative sanctions upto end-March 2000 was 95.45 per cent of the total assistance sanctioned to SSI sector.

Assistance to Backward Districts

The growth of assistance to backward districts during the last five years is reflected in the table-5.4given below:

Table—5.4 Growth of Sanctions & Disbursement of Term Loans to SSI Sector in Backward District *(Kalahandi, Dhenkanal, Keonjhar, Mayurbhanj, Koraput)*

Year	*Sanctions*	*Growth rate (%)*	*Disbursement*	*Growth rate (%)*
1995-96	7.17	–	2.95	–
1996-97	9.06	26.36	6.70	127.12
1997-98	13.57	49.78	5.82	(-) 13.13
1998-99	7.12	(-) 47.53	3.69	(-) 36.60
1999-00	13.52	89.89	7.50	103.25

Source: Annual Reports of OSFC.

It is observed by the above table that the year 1999-2000 witnessed the highest growth (89.89%) in terms of assistance sanctioned to SSI sector in backward district. There was a negative growth in terms of sanction in the year 1998-99. The year 1996-97 witnessed the highest growth rate (127.12%) in terms of assistance disbursed to SSI sector in backward district. The share of backward districts in the total assistance sanctioned to SSI sector was 18.74% during 1999-2000.

Industry-wise Assistance

Industry-wise assistance sanctioned during the last five years is shown in the table-5.5 given below:

Table—5.5 Industry-wise Sanction of Term Loans to SSI Sector

(Rs. Crore)

Sl. No.	*Sector*	*1995-96*	*1996-97*	*1997-98*	*1998-99*	*1999-00*	*Cumulative up to end March 2000*
1.	Food Products	12.02	8.03	14.89	13.01	17.02	130.57
2.	Textiles	0.39	1.84	0.65	1.11	4.87	29.64
3.	Paper & Paper Products	1.79	1.71	0.97	1.59	0.98	16.56
4.	Chemical & Chemical Products	3.66	2.58	2.20	2.85	2.01	69.76
5.	Cement	0.57	1.15	0.89	--	1.5	15.19
6.	Basic metal	2.94	3.54	16.19	2.61.	14.12	55.58
7.	Rubber and rubber products	1.58	4.12	0.19	2.14	4.39	16.65
	Total (including others)	**27.50**	**32.04**	**55.98**	**43.74**	**59.57**	**576.13**

Source: Annual Reports of OSFC.

The above table reveals that food product in the SSI registered the highest share (22.66%) of cumulative assistance upto end-March 2000. The top five industries which received the highest assistance upto end-March 2000 were Food Products (22.66%), Chemical and Chemical Products (12.11%), Basic Metal (9.65%), Textiles (5.14%), Rubber and rubber products (2.89%). Food product industries in the SSI sector registered the highest growth (85.43%) in the year 1997-98. Basic Metal industries in the SSI sector registered the highest growth (441%) in the year 1999-00.

Purpose-wise Assistance

Purpose-wise assistance sanctioned during the last five years is shown in the table-5.6 given below:

Table—5.6 Purpose-wise Sanctions (Effective) to SSI Sector

Sl.No.	*Purpose*	*1995-96*	*1996-97*	*1997-98*	*1998-99*	*1999-00*
1.	New Projects	24.60	26.39	33.74	37.23	51.05
2.	Rehabilitation	0.27	0.30	1.04	0.06	0.49
3.	Others (expansion, modernisation, escalation etc.)	2.63	5.36	21.20	6.45	20.61
	Total	**27.50**	**32.05**	**5.98**	**43.74**	**72.15**

Source: Annual Reports of OSFC.

It is apparent from the above table that the new projects constitute the highest share (70.76%) in the cumulative sanction upto end-March 2000. There was consistency in the growth trend of the assistance to new projects during the last five years. Sanctions for expansion, modernisation, escalation etc. registered the highest growth (295.52%) in 1997-98.

The activities of the corporation in the past 45 years have remained more or less confined to granting of direct loans and advances and the other activities like under-writing foreign exchange loans etc., having a negligible share in its loan portfolio. The share of small scale industries financed by OSFC is not noteworthy except in the year 1997-98. However, the depressing performance in the last 40 years have been out-weighed by its performance in the last 5 years. The high record of its performance in the last 5 years because of the new economic reforms displays its potency as a fully grown-up youth to face any situation and enlarge its business.

6

Women Entrepreneurship and S.S.I. Sector

A Study of O.S.F.C. as a Facilitator

Dr. S.B. Tripathy*

B.K. Dash**

The present paper seek to highlight the position of women entrepreneurs in the field of SSI in the State of Orissa, those who have provided with the finance from Orissa State Financial Corporation (OSFC). Industrialisation is a sina-qua-non for economic development. The small scale industries play a significant role in the process of industrial development of our country. They have a high potential for generating employment, dispersal to semi-urban and rural areas, promoting entrepreneurship and earning foreign exchange.

The concept of development is pluralist and multidimensional by nature. It means increase in the quality of life irrespective of regions, caste, creed and sex. But this philosophy of development is observed more in the breach than in its implementation. We find some states are highly developed than others, some influential people or castes garnering a lion's share of the development than others. But one highly potential but blissfully forgotten agent of

* Reader in Commerce, Dhenkanal College, Dhenkanal.

** Lecturer in Commerce, IMIT, Cuttack.

development is woman. They have one-tenth of the global income. They own 1/100th of the means of production. This alone shows the degree of neglect and gender oppression against women all over the world which includes India. Recognising the need for developing the status of women, the United Nation in the year 1975 declared the Women Development Decade. To correct the gender discrimination the year 2001 was observed in India as the year of Women Empowerment. The Sixth Five Year Plan laid emphasis on raising the employment status of woman. Subsequent Five Year Plans also laid emphasis on the increasing participation of women in the process of development. The Ninth Five Year Plan laid a vigorous emphasis on economic empowerment of women. Among other things the ninth plan document highlighted the need to equip women with necessary skills in the modern upcoming trades which could keep them gainfully engaged besides making them economically independent and self-reliant and to increase access to credit through setting up a 'Development Bank' for women entrepreneurs for small and tiny sector. Under the plan, provisions were also made to provide forward and backward linkage for credit and marketing facilities to women entrepreneurs.

Orissa is one of the most backward states of the country. Its backwardness is generally attributed to the conventional methods of agriculture, high degree of illiteracy, paucity of funds and lack of entrepreneurship. Majority of women in the state are engaged in the daily household chores. This results in engaging a large chunk of human resource in an obscurant unproductive way. The women of developed states like Gujarat, Maharastra and Andhra Pradesh, are engaged in more gainful employment as compared to Orissa. So men in the state need to encourage participating in the process of development.

Different schemes are already there to facilitate the participation of women in the process of development. The Self Help Group (SHG) formulated under DWCRA Scheme is a rudimentary stepping-stone for engaging women in the economic activities. Small scale sector is an ideal area to utilise the untapped talent and skill of women.

Timely availability of finance is a pre-condition for the success of any enterprise. Several institutions provide both long term as well as working capital to SSI sector. Orissa State Finance Corporation (OSFC) is a principal financing institution in the state providing term loan to SSI sector. It was established in the year 1957 in view of the potentiality and the undeniable role, the women entrepreneurs are expected to play in the small scale industrial development of the state, a study of the financing agency like OSFC and the general attitude of such agencies towards women entrepreneurs have become imperative.

Table—6.1 No. of SSI Set-up Women Entrepreneurs with Investment and Employment during 1990-91 to 1997-98

Year	*No. of units*	*Amount of investment (Rs.)*	*Employment (no. of persons)*
1990-91	109 (2249	286.89 (6099.87)	812 (15657)
1991-92	139 (2233)	276.48 (5203.38)	818 (15545)
1992-93	168 (2117)	526.50 (5499.96)	1152 (13344)
1993-94	134 (2311)	357.72 (5620.64)	908 (13807)
1994-95	134 (2327)	335.27 (6808.15)	694 (13096)
1995-96	185 (2507)	592.95 (7481.90)	967 (13019)
1996-97	232 (3098)	840.83 (10452.52)	1280 (15629)
1997-98	216 (3186)	1328.96 (13408.70)	1109 (16716)
Total	**1317 (20028)**	**4545.40 (60575.12**	**7740 (116813)**

Note: (Figures in brackets indicate about total SSI units).

Source: Statistical hand book-1997-98, Directorate of Industries, Orissa.

In Table-6.1 SSI units set up by women entrepreneurs with investment made by them and employment opportunities created during the period 1990-91 to 1997-98 are presented. The Table also depicts the above features for the entire SSI units of the state for the same period. An analysis of the Table exhibits that during 1990-91 to 1997-98, 1,317 SSI units were set up by women entrepreneurs against the total 20,028 units set up in the entire state. Likewise, during the same period against the total investment of Rs. 60,575.12

lakhs the women entrepreneurs have invested Rs. 4545.40 lakhs and had created employment opportunities for 7,740 persons against the total 1,16,813 persons for 7,740 persons against the total 1,16,813 persons for the entire state. Further, the analysis reveals that the SSI units in the entire state which were numbering 2,249 during 1990-91 increased to 3,186 during 1997-98, whereas during the same period SSI units set up by women entrepreneurs have made about two-fold increase. During the same period the investments in the SSI units by women entrepreneurs recorded a remarkable five-fold increase as against a mere two-fold increase in case of total SSI units.

Table—6.2 Assistance Sanctioned by O.S.F.C. to SSI Units During 1990-91 to 1997-98

Year	*No. of SSI units*	*Amount (Rs. in lakhs)*	*No. of SSI units set-up by Women Entrepreneurs*	*Amount (Rs. in lakhs)*
1990-91	456	2729.93	15	52.49
1991-92	299	1983.55	6	22.85
1992-93	252	2683.04	9	20.16
1993-94	226	2114.41	13	34.32
1994-95	137	1596.27	4	10.27
1995-96	180	2749.86	10	17.54
1996-97	221	3204.36	16	69.13
1997-98	357	5598.07	38	242.07
Total	**2128**	**22659.49**	**111**	**468.83**

Source: Annual Reports of OSFC - 1990-91 to 1997-98.

In Table-6.2 assistance sanctioned by OSFC to SSI units in the state during 1990-91 to 1997-98 are shown. A review of the Table indicates that an amount of Rs. 22,659.49 lakhs was sanctioned by OSFC to 2128 SSI units during 1990-91 to 1997-98. During the same period 111 SSI units set up by women entrepreneurs have received Rs. 468.83 lakhs from OSFC. The analysis further adds that on an average, while the assistant of OSFC per SSI unit is Rs. 10.65 lakhs, in case of SSI unit set up by women entrepreneurs, it is against the total investment by SSI units of Rs. 60,575,12 laksh (Table-6.1), assistance sanctioned by OSFC is Rs. 22,659,49 lakhs, i.e. 37.4%, whereas against the total investment of Rs. 4545.40 lakhs by SSI set up by women entrepreneurs the Corporation's assistance is only Rs. 468.83 lakhs i.e. 10.31%.

It can be inferred from the above observations that the women entrepreneurs have better potentiality to set up new SSI units in the state. This is corroborated from the above analysis in terms of increase in number of units and amount invested in the period under review. Unfortunately, the assistance rendered by OSFC does not match to the potentiality of women entrepreneurs, as there is a huge gap between the assistance extended to SSI units in general and SSI units set up by women entrepreneurs. Therefore, it is very much imperative on the part of the corporation to modify its strategy to escalate its assistance in favour of women entrepreneurs for the rapid economic development of the state.

The women are critical to the process of making their families out of poverty. The participation of women in business and for that matter their economic empowerment is not just another economic activity. It can bring radical transformation in the socio-economic conditions of our society. Prevalence of patriarchy norms and stereotype gender bias has kept a major chunk of human resource in a state of oblivion. The financial improvement of women i.e., their accessibility to savings and credit facilities would improve gender economic status. The attitude of the financial institutions in providing financial assistance to women entrepreneurs should change. As of now the accessibility of women to savings and credit from banking and non-banking financial institutes is meagre and abysmally low particularly in case of rural women.

7

Financing of Small Scale Industries by Commercial Banks in Orissa

A Study

Sri Sudhansu Kumar Das*

Dr. Bimal Prasad Nanda**

Introduction

Orissa is one of the least developed states of India. Orissa comprising 4.74 per cent of the India's landmass and with 31.66 million of people as per 1991 census accounts for 3.74 per cent of the total population of the country. About 87 per cent of its population live in rural areas and depend on agriculture and allied activities for their livelihood. Orissa, despite being a land of exquisite art, craft, architecture, rich culture and maritime heritage, large mineral deposits including precious stones and wide coastline, has been wading through unending poverty and unemployment. The economy of the state is characterised by low per capita income, low capital base, slow economic growth, alarming external debt, inadequate exploitation of natural resources and poor infrastructure.

* Lecturere in Commerce, S.G. College, East Jajpur.

** Reader in Commerce, Govt. College, Anugul.

The most pressing need of developing a country is rapid industrialisation, in order to be able to achieve the basic objectives of its economic and social progress. It has been recognised that industrialisation is the surest solution to the problem of a rising the standard of living of the people.[1]

The small scale industries (SSIs) are viewed increasingly an important vehicle for meeting both growth and equity objectives of developing economics including Orissa. For economic development of any country, SSIs have a crucial role to play. Keeping this in view, a well-organised institutional structure has been created to meet the credit need of this sector, which consists of Commercial Banks, Regional Rural Banks (RRBs), Co-operatives and State Financial Corporations (SFCs). While commercial banks, co-operative and regional rural banks provide particularly working capital, the state financial corporations meet the block capital requirement of this sector. At the apex level, Small Industrial Development Bank of India (SIDBI) provide refinance and co-ordinate the activities of these institutions engaged in providing credit need to this sector. Besides, NABARD also provide refinance assistance to this sector.[2]

In this paper, an attempt is made to study the contribution of commercial banks in financing small scale industries in the state and inter-district disparity in the distribution of bank credit of commercial banks to SSI sector.

Growth and Development

After independence, a number of institutional agencies were set up by the government to provide credit need of SSI sector. Among these, commercial banks emerged as the prime source of institutional credit to this sector. The importance banks as supplier of credit to SSI sector further increased because of many initiatives taken by successive governments and virtually a dormant money market in the country.

The role of commercial banks in providing financial assistance to this sector further accelerated after nationalisation of banks. There has been a substantial growth of bank credit of commercial banks to this sector. The sector analysis of advance of commercial banks reveals that, aggregate advance to this sector has increased from

Rs. 528 lakhs in 1972 (which was 16.1 per cent of total advance of industrial sector) to Rs. 16,752 lakhs in 1986 (which was 29.1 per cent of total advance to industrial sector).[3]

Keeping in view the rapid growth of small scale industries in the state, the state government has taken many important measures. Following are a few of these:

1. Establishment of District Industry Centres (DICs) in all districts of the state.
2. Change in the Industrial Policy of the government heavily weighted in favour of small and cottage industries.
3. Opening of branches of Orissa State Financial Corporation (OSFC) in District headquarters.
4. Rapid branch expansion of commercial banks particularly in unbanked and rural centres.

The DICs acted as a catalytic agent in promoting SSIs through generation of project ideas and identification of new entrepreneurs. The sanction of number of incentives and subsidies by the state government and financing of a large number of small sector units by the OSFC resulted in a big boost to industrial financing to small industries sector.

Real boost to institutional financing to SSI came during post-reform period. In response to financial sector reform. The state government reformulated its industrial policy in March 1996 with a view to improve the investment climate in the state and promoting opportunities for growth of industries and related activities. New Industrial Policy of 1996 emphasised the development of SSIs in the state. In the new organisational and structural set up, the District Industry Centres (DICs) operate as nodal agency for development of SSIs and recommending various incentives. Also government took positive measures in this regard like setting up DICs in newly created districts, provisioning for water, power and other industries friendly infrastructure.[4]

Growth and development of small scale industries in Orissa in term of number of units, investment and generation of employment during the period 1994-95 and 1999-00 is presented in the table-7.1.

Table—7.1 Growth and Development of SSIs in Orissa

Sl. No.	Year	No. of SSI units set up	Investment (Rs. in crores)	Employment Generation (No. of persons)
1.	By the end of 94-95	47104	729.58	336781
2.	95-96	2507	74.82	13019
3.	96-97	3098	104.53	15629
4.	97-98	3186	134.09	16716
5.	98-99	3184	190.06	16776
6.	99-00	3473	162.94	18608
7.	By the end of 99-00	62552	1396.02	417529

Source: Director of Industries, Orissa, Cuttack.

Table-7.1 shows that there is positive growth of SSI units in the state in all respects. The total number of small industries has increased from 47104 units in 1994-95 to 62552 units in 1999-00, which is 32.8 per cent increase between the two periods. At the same time, total investment has registered an increase of 91.35 per cent between the said periods.

The credit provided to SSIs Commercial Banks, Regional Rural Bank, Co-operatives and Orissa State Financial Corporation in the state during the period of March 1991 to March 2000 under annual credit plan is presented in the table-7.2.

Table—7.2 Institution-wise Financing to Small Scale Industries in Orissa

(Rs. in lakhs)

Year (as on)	Commercial Banks	RRBs	Co-operatives	OSFC	Total advance
1	2	3	4	5	6
March 91	1432.66 (20.66)	144.37 (2.08)	387.58 (5.59)	4970.47 (71.67)	6935.08 (100.00)
March 92	2547.80 (42.86)	229.82 (3.87)	643.77 (10.83)	2522.96 (42.44)	5944.35 (100.00)
March 93	2502.05 (58.34)	145.24 (3.39)	1.94 (0.045)	1639.37 (38.22)	4288.60 (100.00)

(Table Contd...)

1	2	3	4	5	6
March 94	2835.31 (67.37)	344.21 (8.810)	–	1028.84 (24.45)	4208.36 (100.00)
March 95	3731.68 (59.32)	578.40 (09.2)	1640.11 (26.08)	339.63 (5.4)	6288.82 (100.00)
March 96	5485.04 (62.83)	565.82 (06.48)	1059.96 (12.14)	1618.81 (18.55)	8729.63 (100.00)
March 97	6617.23 (53.33)	946.20 (07.63)	1910.11 (15.39)	2934.00 (23.65)	12407.54 (100.00)
March 98	7282.94 (45.7)	1245.08 (07.8)	3155.07 (19.8)	4262.00 (6.7)	15935.00 (100.00)
March 99	8718.78 (50.25)	1343.93 (07.74)	2584.58 (14.89)	4705.00 (27.12)	17352.27 (100.00)
March 00	9653.00 (56.65)	1020.00 (05.99)	1375.00 (08.07)	4790.00 (29.29)	17036.00 (100.00)

Note: 1. Figures in bracket are percentage of total.
2. Amount represents in lakhs.

Source: Various issues of Agenda Note, Annual Credit Plan, State Level Bankers committiees, UCO Bank, Orissa, Bhubaneswar.

It is clear from table-7.2 that there is substantial growth of credit by commercial banks both in term of volume and share to total institutions finance to SSI sector. Commercial banks advance has registered an increase of about 6.7 times over the period from March 1990 to March 2000. Also the share of commercial banks advance to total institutional advance has considerably increased from 20.67 per cent in March 91 to 56.65 per cent in March 2000. At the same time, the share of Orissa State Financial Corporation has reduced to 29.29 per cent in March 2000 from a high of 71.67 per cent in March 91. It is clear from the above analysis that commercial banks has played a dominant role in meeting the credit need of small industries in the state.

Inter District Disparity

It is disturbing to note that along with increasing share of commercial banks credit to SSIs, in the state, there exists the later district disparity in the distribution of credit. The increasing dose of bank credit to the SSI sector has been concentrated to few industrially developed districts of the state. Table-7.3 depicts the distribution of bank credit to SSIs in different districts of the state as on 31st March 2000.

Table—7.3 Distribution of Bank Credit of Scheduled Commercial Banks to SSIs in different districts of Orissa

(Rs. in Thousand)

Sl. No.	*Name of the Districts*	*Name of Accounts*	*Outstanding Credit (as on 31st March 2000)*	*% to state total*
1	*2*	*3*	*4*	*5*
1.	Angul	4436	88980	1.41
2.	Balasore	6340	358903	7.55
3.	Bargarh	5372	191848	4.035
4.	Bhadrak	3437	121239	2.55
5.	Bolangir	6089	81310	1.71
6.	Boudh	1634	28536	0.60
7.	Cuttack	14531	523615	10.99
8.	Deogarh	349	4727	0.10
9.	Dhenkanal	8462	149725	3.14
10.	Gajapati	1034	2.114	0.42
11.	Ganjam	6686	206693	4.345
12.	Jagatsinghpur	3699	66385	1.39
13.	Jajpur	7900	107915	2.27
14.	Jharsuguda	1115	47330	0.99
15.	Kalahandi	11949	131422	2.76
16.	Kandhmal	2702	28944	0.61
17.	Kendrapara	5177	60418	1.27
18.	Keonjhar	5054	79030	1.66
19.	Khurda	12404	564931	11.87
20.	Koraput	6072	91310	1.92
21.	Malkangiri	1818	14622	0.31
22.	Mayurbhanj	20499	239614	5.04
23.	Nuapara	3060	30338	0.64
24.	Nawarangpur	2883	31848	0.67
25.	Nayagarh	2829	40392	0.85
26.	Puri	–	354070	7.43
27.	Rayagada	2648	30401	0.64

(Table Contd...)

1	2	3	4	5
28.	Sambalpur	3509	560626	11.78
29.	Sonepur	3759	34408	0.72
30.	Sundargarh	6424	494808	10.40
	Total	–	**4762502**	–

Note: 1. Amount represents in thousands.

2. Small Scale Industries include artisan and village industries.

Source: Basic Statistical return, District-wise classification of outstanding credit of scheduled commercial banks according to occupation. Reserve Bank of India, Mumbai, March 2000, Vol. 29.

Table-7.3 shows that districts like Deogarh, Malkangiri, Boudh, Gajapati and many others are extremely credit deficit districts. Whereas Cuttack, Khurda, Sambalpur, Sundergarh are credit surplus districts as credit supply is much more than their respective contribution to SSI output.

By the end of March 2000, nine districts out of the total thirty districts of the state like Cuttack, Khurda, Sambalpur, Sundergarh, Puri, Ganjam, Balasore, Bargarh and Mayurbhanj enjoy about 73 per cent of the total outstanding credit of all scheduled commercial banks in the state. On the other hand the rest twenty-one districts enjoy only twenty-seven per cent of the total outstanding credit of scheduled commercial banks. It is also estimated that districts like Khurda, Sambalpur and Sundergarh individually enjoy outstanding credit of scheduled commercial banks which is equal to the outstanding credit of about fifteen industrial backward districts of the state.

Study also shows a variation in distribution of bank credit among the districts in term of their location. Among the coastal districts, credit distribution is poor to the districts like Jajpur, Bhadrak, Jagatsingpur and Kendrapara. Among the tribal district a few industrially sound districts like Sambalpur and Sundargarh enjoy adequate bank credit of scheduled commercial banks.

Conclusion

The above study instructs to role that commercial banks are the important source of finance to small scale industries in the state.

Undoubtedly, they have established a milestone in financing the small scale units. At the same time there has been substantial variation across districts in the distribution of bank credit of scheduled commercial banks to SSI sector. This disparity in the distribution of bank credit is a true challenge to the regional economic development of the state.

There is all to be done by commercial banks in financing small scale industries in the state. It is suggested that opening of specialised branches in the credit deficit districts with a special thrust on financing micro-enterprises would ensure increased flow of bank credit to this sector. However, in the long run flow of bank credit largely depend upon favourable infrastructure and support service to SSIs. Therefore, it is essential that commercial banks should take these aspects into account while framing plans and programmes to augment the flow of credit and reducing disparity.

REFERENCES

1. Sharma, C.P.; *Industrialisation and Regional Development*. Deep and Deep Publication, New Delhi, p. 20.
2. Ramesha, K; Bank Credit to SSI Sector :- A Study in Inter-state Disparity, *Prajnan*, Vol-XXVII, No. 3, 1998-99, NIBM, Pune, p. 281.
3. SLBC, *Various Issues of Agenda Note,* Orissa, UCO Bank, Bhubaneswar.
4. Planning and Co-ordination Dept. Govt. of Orissa, *Economic Survey* 2000-2001, Chapter -9, p. 1 & 10.

8

Institutional Financing for Small Scale Industrial Development of Orissa

A Study of OSFC Berhampur Branch

Prafulla Chandra Mohanty*

Introduction

Small Scale Sector: Small Scale Sector plays an important and crucial role in the economic upliftment of a country. Contribution of this sector in terms of National income, industrial output, export, employment, development of backward areas, strengthening entrepreneurial culture and using the home talents are of immense value.

Small sector is identified in terms of fixed capital investment. All industrial units with a capital investment (on plant and machinery) of not more than rupees one crore are, at present (1999-2000), treated as small scale units. For ancillary units (i.e. those supplying components etc., to large capital industries and the export oriented units) the limit of capital investment is also rupees one crore. Industrial units with an investment of upto Rs. 25 lakhs belong to tiny sector. As on 31st March, 1998, the number of SSI units in the country was Rs. 31.14 lakhs generating employment for

---

* **Senior Faculty Member, Department of Commerce, Aska Science College, Aska, Ganjam.**

167.20 lakhs persons. The value of production aggregated to Rs. 4,65,171 crores, contributing nearly 40% to the country's total industrial production and 35% to India's total exports. By and large such an impressive performance of small scale sector has been made possible due to ceaseless efforts of State Financial Corporations and other financial institutions. The product range is over 7500 items generally produced by this sector. Small scale sector covers a whole gamut of small enterprises.

State Financial Corporations: The SFCs Act, 1951 was enacted by the Parliament close on the heels of Industrial Policy Resolution of 1948. The Act envisaged creation of State Financial Corporation to cater to the non-banking long-term financial need of the intending industrial borrowers. With the objective of promotion economic growth, balanced regional development and widening of entrepreneurial base by financing small enterprises, the SFCs were set up in different states in late fifties. Now onwards, these SFCs are an integral part of the country's financial system. Operation at the grass root level, these developed financial institutions have played a significant role in bringing about decentralised economic development of backward regions and reductions in regional imbalances. The SFCs have played a very crucial role in the promotion of first generation entrepreneurs. As a result, the country has witnessed massive growth in industrial sector, wherein, the role of SFCs have been phenomenal not only in working as a catalyst but also for dispersal of assistance through the length and breadth of this great country. The combined assets of the eighteen State Financial Corporations of the country at the end of March, 2000 stands at Rs. 15,149,14 crores. Out of this Rs. 11,084 crores as loan and advances as much as Rs. 5,777,13 crores (may likely to cross Rs. 6,000 crores on 2000-2001) were becoming non-performing assets which comes to nearly 50.31% of the total or more.

SSIs and OSFC

As a sequel to the establishment of State Financial Corporation, the Orissa State Financial Corporation came into being in the year 1955-1956 which has been harnessing the industrial growth of Orissa by extending term lending facilities to industrial entrepreneurs. Till to date, the Head office of Orissa State Financial Corporation is situated at Cuttack and has six regional offices situated at Cuttack, Bhubaneswar, Balasore, Sambalpur, Bhawanipatna and Berhampur. The Berhampur Regional Office controls the branch OSFC activities of Phulbani, Jayapore, Rayagada and of the Berhampur Branch. The important core strength is the availability of large pool of skilled and qualified hands comprising 40 engineers, a dozen. Chartered and Cost Accountants and MBAs, and a host of experienced managerial and willing work force to manage the show of OSFC nicely in the State of Orissa. It has got the edge over other financial institutional in understanding the pulse of industrial needs of investors because of its sheer long working experience. It has branch networking in district Head quarters and in important business growth centres of the state so as to cater to the credit needs of the investors at their doorsteps. OSFC, till to-day remained the only prime lending institution which spearheaded in extending financial assistance to tiny and small scale industrial units. The performance of the small scale sector of the state and the role of OSFC can be visualised from the following table.

Table—8.1 SSIs of the state

(Rs. in Lakhs)

Year	*SSIs (State)*	*Investments (in Rs.)*	*Employments (in Nos.)*	*SSIs of OSFC Assistance*	*Investments of OSFC*	*% (No)*	*% (Amount)*
1991	38,094	496,56.77	39875	24618	40215.62	64.62	80.99
2000	62,530	1394,32.10	417483	30316	57613.16	48.48	41.32

Source: Directorate of Industries.

The table itself speaks about the role of OSFC in industrialising the state along with other private and public sector banks. With the opening up of economy since 1991, the share of OSFC has drastically reduced from 64.62% to 48.48% in number of units and from 80.99% to 41.32% in amount of investment which is not a sign of efficiency for the working of the OSFC in the state.

The plan wise planned investments in small scale sector of the country has been stated in a table. It is seen that from the first plan period to the 9th plan period the data are plotted which gives an understanding that different governments of India invests more and more funds on small scale sector till the end of 8th plan. Rs. 42 crore investment was increased to 6334 crore rupees during the period of 46 years of planned growth. But the investment in current 9th plan period is somehow less by 1826 crore rupees which is about 20% low. This seems that under the era of financial reforms government gives more chances to the private financing organisation to place money in expanding the business of SSS units.

Table—8.2 Plan-wise investment in Small Scale Sector

(Rs. in Crore)

Name of the Plan	*Investment in Crore*	*Per annum investment (Average)*
1st Plan	42	8.40
2nd Plan	187	37.40
3rd Plan (1966-69)	241	48.20
4th Plan	243	48.60
5th Plan	592	118.40
6th Plan	1945	389.00
7th Plan	3249	649.80
8th Plan	6334	1266.80
9th Plan (1997-2002)	4508	901.60
Total Investment	17467	73.13

Source: *Indian Economy*, A.N. Agrawala, 27th Edn. 2001 p. 389.

In the above National and State small scale sector scenario, the present paper also tries to study the performance of OSFC in financing small scale industries of Ganjam district through its Berhampur Branch which was established since 1976. The study is basically limited to its amounts of sanction, disbursement and outstanding the data used for the study are mostly secondary collected from various issues of annual reports and other timely publications of the Government and of the corporation.

Berhampur Branch and its Industrial Development Activities

Ganjam district having 31,36,937 strong population (as per 2001 census) is one of the most populous districts in the state. Every geographical square kilometre area of the district inhabitants 382 persons of population. The major industries in the district are M/s. Indian Rare Earths Ltd., Aska Sugar, Jayshree Chemicals Ltd., etc. However, in the field of industrial growth the district did not make any sufficient contribution as yet. OSFC by establishing a brand at Berhampur since 1976 tries to achieve industrial growth of the area. Berhampur alternatively named, as the silk city has been the point of attraction in the whole of South Orissa. The people mostly here are tradesmen and there are few pockets who account for the industrial sector. Ganjam with a rich natural endowment and has got lots of potentialities for industrial growth as well. Nevertheless, the effort of Berhampur Branch has been phenomenal to moot the idea of industrialisation which has taken decided proportions in the form of promotional activities in the industrial estate. A score of cozy and comfortable hotels, well set of nursing homes, other industrial houses and a large fleet of passenger and cargo carriers were set off by the endeavour of this branch. The branch has success stories on agro based industries by upbringing modern rice mills, dal mills, cashew processing units, etc. Similarly, some secondary steel and chemical industries also have record performance.

Findings

The branch has completed 25 years of service on last 15th February, 2001. During the period of the branch has triggered off from 37 operating accounts involving Rs. 21.79 lakhs in the year of start, (1976) has now risen to high echelons of 1400 operating accounts involving Rs. 6000 lakhs. It is remarkable to point out that over these years of operation, the branch has assisted 900 numbers of Small Road Transport Operators (SRTOS), 1200 numbers of SSIs has generated employment opportunity for 50,000 people directly and more on indirectly.

The financial activities of the OSFC, Berhampur Branch are plotted in an annexure which gives information the amount sanctioned, disbursed, recovered and outstanding amount for the year of inception. Regarding the volume of business increase, it is seen that in the amount sanctioned has risen by 11 times, disbursement by 39 times and outstanding amount by 41/2 times whereas the operating accounts increased from 68 Nos. to 1291 i.e. 20 times during the period. On calculating per account sanction over the period the amount has been fallen from 1.1 lakh rupees to 0.63 lakh rupees. Similarly, the disbursement has risen from 0.34 lakhs to 0.61 lakhs rupees and so outstanding from 0.6 lakhs to 2.5 lakhs rupees during this period of 26 years of operation.

The average amounts per annum is also calculated and seen that the branch has sanctioned nearly 3.11 lakh rupees to 801 accounts but disbursed 2.40 lakh rupees which accumulates an yearly outstanding of 130 lakh rupees. It is seen from the study that the financing activities of the branch is gradually paralysed due to the accumulation of the over dues represented by the increasing outstanding.

Conclusion

In the era of industrial development, the role of OSFC and its Berhampur Branch is to play an important role mostly in establishing, financing, nourishing the small scale units. But in Orissa, the prosperity of establishing small scale industrial units are being pressed up by the misuse of finance, increase of sick units, low recovery rates and high rate of outstanding amounts which carry the risk of non-performing assets. Along with this, the State Financial Corporation also reaps the evils of liberalisation of the economy and competition from the side of banking and other financial institutions. Besides this, the progress of Berhampur Branch seems to be very slow and the people have no entrepreneurial zeal which is required for the accelerating the activities in the district. In the light of the above conclusion some suggestions can be drawn for the better performance of OSFC Berhampur branch. The efficiency of working of the branch are below 60%. So the units should be ready to 100% efficient. The units which are sick they may thoroughly be surveyed for survival or otherwise they are to be closed. Some more industrial climate in rural and semi-urban areas. It is necessary to find new policies of debt recovery by which the outstanding burden of the corporation can be lessened and so the corporation will get more strength to provide more funds by recycling its funds. At the last but not the least the Government should come with new policies in equalising the collection and disbursement interest rates for all financing institutions in the country without making any difference as is now persists between the banking institutions and the State Financial Corporations.

ANNEXURE—I

Orissa State Financial Corporation Berhampur Branch
Comparative Performance in last 25 years

(Rs. in lakh)

Year	*Sanction*	*Disburse*	*Recovery*	*No. of A/c*	*Outstanding*
Up to 75	61.55	36.88	00	37	21.79
1975-76	73.90	23.05	28.32	68	41.28
1976-77	21.28	18.66	34.66	90	61.44
1977-78	28.68	26.47	31.32	102	71.42
1978-79	101.55	34.8	38.57	145	86.42
1979-80	127.93	68.00	47.52	210	124.57
1980-81	166.29	106.63	52.35	321	284.31
1981-82	153.64	135.68	81.65	515	376.4
1982-83	152.18	104.27	59.55	563	468.68
1983-84	291.74	175.07	108	622	585.58
1984-85	320.62	166.76	115	682	720.92
1985-86	397.64	232.91	132.37	741	898.88
1986-87	318.01	274.68	191.88	847	1085.22
1987-88	282.55	308.64	259.75	920	1234.15
1988-89	269.49	263.02	245.89	949	1376.37
1989-90	421.65	216.26	303.86	976	1460.21
1990-91	442.27	333.88	258.37	1038	1651.32
1991-92	260.04	328.33	288.76	1064	1782.48
1992-93	273.15	219.08	349.84	1076	1975.54
1993-94	161.46	256.81	314.1	1098	2274.70
1994-95	241.37	193.94	263.45	1101	2360.21
1995-96	721.37	380.29	275.52	1081	2632.24
1996-97	524.77	383.86	524.57	1100	2801.02
1997-98	302.53	289.77	417.98	1113	2879.26
1998-99	409.08	237.45	353.41	1134	2977.05
1999-2k	592.84	453.69	321.76	1169	3108.98
2k-2001	806.68	789.03	606.41	1291	3291.60

REFERENCES

1. *Indian Economy*, 27th Edn., 2001, Agrawala A.N.
2. Annual Report of OSFC.
3. Souvenir Silver Jubilee (1976-2001) of Orissa State Financial Corporation, Berhampur Branch, Berhampur.
4. *Indian Economy*, Dhingra Edn., 1999.
5. *Orissa Review* March, 2001 Issue, I & PR Department, Government of Orissa.
6. *Indian Journal of Commerce*, December, 2000 Issue.

9

Non-farm Sector Investment in Selected Districts of Orissa

An Impact Assessment

Sri Ramesh Chandra Jena*
Dr. Pitabasha Mohanty**
Dr. R.K. Nanda***

Development of non-farm sector (NFS) assumes great importance in the context of limited capacity of the farm sector in generating employment opportunities for the growing rural work force. The thrust area status accorded to NFS signifies the importance, which the NABARD has attached, to be development of this sector. The NABARD with a view to promoting overall rural development, has been playing an important role in the development of NFS activities in the rural and semi-urban areas by extending refinance support to the credit institutions for financing these activities. During 1985-86 the NABARD introduced the Automatic Refinance Facility (ARF) Schemes, viz. Composite Loan Scheme and Integrated Loan Scheme. Under the former scheme, loan up to a maximum of Rs. 50000[1] was provided to individual artisans and small entrepreneurs for meeting the block and/or working capital requirement while under the latter scheme, loan up to Rs. 10 lakh[2] was provided to

* Sr. Lecturer in Commerce, Kendrapara College, Kendrapara.
** Sr. Lecturer in Commerce, Kendrapara College, Kendrapara.
*** Reader in Commerce, SCS (Autonomous) College, Puri.

individuals, group of individuals, partnership concerns and industrial cooperatives for meeting the requirements of block as well as working capital for one operating cycle[3]. In order to assess the impact of financing NFS investments on income and employment generation, an attempt is made here to study the sample units of two districts of Orissa. The present paper is an abridged version of the said study.

Objectives

The specific objectives of the study are:

1. To examine the systems and procedures adopted by different financing agencies in the appraisal of loan applications, their sanctions and disbursement.
2. To assess the adequacy or otherwise of credit support, both for meeting the working capital and block capital requirement.
3. To estimate the costs and benefits from the investments in non-farm activities.
4. To estimate the employment generation from the selected activities.
5. To study the repayment performance of the sample beneficiaries and
6. To assess the extent and effectiveness of linkages with special reference to inputs availability, technical guidance, marketing of products, training facilities etc.

Methodology

Two districts accounting for a considerable share of the total refinance disbursed under NFS by the NABARD for example undivided Cuttack and Puri were selected for the conduct of impact assessment study. Out of the predominant financing agency in each of these two districts of one or two banks was done, on the basis of maximum availment of refinance for NFS activities. Major activities accounting for maximum number of beneficiaries and maximum disbursement and major bank branches, which had financed these activities, were identified. Altogether 16 bank branches and 198 sample beneficiaries were selected for the study. The reference year being July 2000 to June 2001. Data collected from the sample beneficiaries related to cost of investment, level of production realized, cost of production, gross income, net income, generation of employment, etc. and those collected from the records maintained by the selected bank branches were on purpose of loan, amount of loan, dates of loan application, repayment performance, etc. Branch Managers of selected banks and officials of concerned development agencies were also interviewed to understand problems and prospects of development of selected activities in each district.

Scheme Implementation

1. The rate of interest charged by the branches of commercial banks varied from 12 to 15% per annum, i.e., higher by two to five percentage points than the stipulated rate.
2. The moratorium period for repayment of loans fixed by the banks was generally shorter than the minimum of 12 months stipulated by the NABARD.
3. As against the NABARD's stipulated repayment period ranging from a minimum period of three years to a maximum period of 10 years, the repayment period fixed by the bank branches ranged from as 25 months (Rope making in Puri district) to as long as 132 months (Carpentry in Cuttack district).
4. 14% of the sample borrowers were observed to have misutilised the loan amount either fully or partly. The main reasons for misutilisation were (A) inadequacy of loan amount, (B) poor returns from investments due to lack of adequate infrastructure facilities for supply of raw materials and marketing of products, etc.
5. At the bank level, coordination between banks and Districts Industries Centre (DIC) was not taken before sanctioning of the loan.

Cost of Investment and Financing

The adequacy of loan to meet block and working capital requirements presented a mixed bag. Under financing of block capital was pronounced in the case of motor winding (52%) and furniture making (48%) brick making in Cuttack district leather works (30%) and painting (30%) in Puri district. It was observed that the beneficiaries had mostly made good the short-fall by borrowing from other sources. In the case of working capital, there was large scale. Under financing for wood painting works and leather works (52%) in Puri district and motor binding works (73%) brick making (66%) in Cuttack district.

Over financing of block capital was observed in the case of tailoring (91%) in Cuttack district. In case of working capital, the over financing observed was of a small magnitude in absolute terms and was of a very high order in relative terms in the case of hand fan- making (350%), tailoring (222%), rope making (114%) in Cuttack district.

Lack of realistic appraisal by the bank branches resulted in improper assessment of the duration of the operating cycle as well as the actual requirement of block and working capital. This had resulted in either over financing or under financing by the bank branches.

Economies of NFS Investments

Availability of institutional financing/credit encouraged the rural artisans and the SSI units to expand or take up traditional activity on their own for raising their level of income. The institutional credit brought about desirable shift from wage employment to self-employment especially for women in the area of our study.

Considering the wide variation in cost of investment comprising the block and working capital (for one operating cycle) the net income per Rs. 100 of investment varied from Re.1 (leather work) in Puri to a high level of Rs. 333 hand fan-making in Cuttack district. Capital intensive activities included leather works units (producing purses, school bags etc.) furniture making and painting on cloth/wood etc. for which the return per Rs. 100 of investment was low. On the other hand, activities like hand fan-making, rope-making tailoring etc. were relatively less capital intensive and in these cases the income per Rs. 100 of investment was quite high. The capital intensive brick manufacturing activity generated considerable income (Rs. 52 to Rs. 167) and gainful employment per Rs. 100 of investment (6-7 person days).

In the case of traditional leather activities like shoe/chapal making and leather tanning, average net income realized varied from Rs. 4193 (Puri) to Rs. 15675 (Cuttack) depending upon the scale of operation and level of investment. In Puri district, however, the marginal negative net returns suggested that the activity provided only assured self-employment to the family members at market rates for a reasonable duration in a year. Further, the commercial leather activity pursued by a group borrowers in Puri district with support of voluntary agency, which helped in procuring raw materials, providing designs, training and marketing outlet enabled the borrowers to realise net income of Rs. 44651. The basic element of provision of linkages by the voluntary agencies needs to be emulated by DICs in their respective districts.

Rope making activities pursued in Cuttack and Puri districts and hand fan-making units in Cuttack were supplementary in nature and generated employment opportunities for about 3-10 months in a year. Depending upon the level of technology used for rope making (manual/wooden/iron twisting) and duration of work, the net income varied from Rs. (-) 909 to Rs. 3249. The middlemen influenced, to a large extent, the supply of raw materials and marketing of rope. Establishment of integrated cooperatives for the benefit of rope making units may help to break the stronghold of private traders, thereby ensuing better returns to the beneficiaries.

Despite high wage rates and labour-intensive nature of the activity the net income was positive and ranged from (Rs. 25778 in Puri to Rs. 60025 in Cuttack district for brick making due to boom in construction activity and surging demand for bricks after the super cyclone of Oct. 1999.

Among the other activities, impact for financing for tailoring and garment making units was uneven in the study areas depending upon the scale of operation. Identification of beneficiaries in Puri was not based on the entrepreneurial ability in many cases, which in turn reduced the profitability of investment (Rs. 8071). Financing for sewing and interlocking machines in Cuttack enabled the beneficiaries to realize relatively higher income (Rs. 4243) than the beneficiaries financed for sewing machine alone (Rs. 3056).

Employment Generation

The impact of investment in NFS activities on employment generation was uneven across the activities and also the activities of the same group within the district depending upon the nature of activity, level of investment and the scale of operation. The creation of non-recurring employment was almost negligible. Seasonal activities like brick making activity, which generated employment of 3530 person days in Cuttack. The brick manufacturing activity created employment especially for the hired labour (87 per cent)

Repayment Performance

The repayment performance of the sample beneficiaries was not satisfactory as the percentage of overdue to demand worked out to 52. It was observed that the percentage of overdue to demand varied from 16 in Puri to as high as 76 in Cuttack. Further the repayment performance in Puri was quite good while it is not satisfactory in Cuttack District. Among the activities the percentage of overdue to demand ranged from about 10 to 13 in the case of brick manufacturing, shoe making (operating cycle 30 days), rope making and furniture making activities to 95 per cent. Incidence of very high overdue (about 76 per cent) was observed among beneficiaries engaged in brick making, furniture making in Cuttack district financed by DCCB, tailoring in Cuttack district financed by UCO Bank. Comparison of annual debt service liabilities with net income indicated that these default were wilful as less then 50 percentage of the net income was required for servicing the debt.

Development of Linkages

The availability of raw material, in adequate quantity, for efficient running of the sample units was not a problem as reported by the borrower. However, the raw material for the leather activity was procured from far off places, even from outside the state.

The various equipment and tools necessary for setting up and running the units were locally available. The voluntary agency in Puri district was even providing the designs, pattern and had also arranged for training of the beneficiaries.

Majority of the sample borrowers reported that availability of labour was not a problem as they were pursuing traditional activities and family labour was generally employed. In the case of brick manufacturing units in Cuttack it was reported that contractual arrangement for labour was a common practice.

The NFS activities covered under the study were traditional in nature and as most of the sample beneficiaries were already engaged in these activities, they were fully conversant with the technique of operation. Twenty per cent of the sample beneficiaries of leatherwork in Puri district had received training at Central Leather Research Institute, Madras for 3 months due to the efforts of a Voluntary Agency in the area. None of the remaining sample beneficiaries had reported having undergone training for taking up these activities. Adequate arrangement for providing formal training for rural artisan would also be helpful in the development of NFS activities. This would not only enable the borrowers to enhance the scale of operation for the traditional activities being pursued by them but would also encourage them in adoption of latest technology.

Although no institutional arrangements for marketing of products were available, borrowers did not report any difficulties in marketing of their products. For the beneficiaries who were producing fancy items like leather bags, purses, etc. their goods were sold in trade fairs organized at Bhubaneswar, Cuttack, Delhi, Bombay etc. However, prevalence of lower margin of profit in some cases and resorting job work indicate implicit marketing stress.

The major problem faced by the rural artisan and other entrepreneurs related to inadequacy of infrastructural facilities such as roads, water, electricity etc.

Policy Issues

The appraisal of the loan applications by the bank staff not being appropriate resulted often in sanction of unrealistic loan amounts and calls for appropriate action on the part of the concerned officials.

A comprehensive system of regular monitoring and supervision needs to be evolved to ensure proper end use of the loan amount and to minimize of misutilisation of loans.

The role of the DIC in identification of the beneficiaries of non-farm sector activities and in guiding the banks in appraising in the loan applications being negligible calls for a better co-ordination among the financing banks, the DIC and other development agencies at the district level. The findings of the study bring out the need for establishing integrated co-operative, which may break the stronghold of the private traders, thereby ensuring better returns to the beneficiaries.

Inadequate infrastructural support in terms of lack of facilities such as water, power, roads and marketing resulted in the borrowers earning less than the anticipated income. While financial support would be available for the non-farm sector activities from the banks, the government will have to ensure provision of these necessary inputs for success of the activities. The involvement of NGOs in providing training, arranging for supply of raw materials and marketing of finished products would improve the success rate of the non-farm sector activities.

High level of overdue and their wilful nature suggest the need for concerted steps on the part of financing banks to improve recovery performance under NFS activities.

As the phenomenon of overcharging interest to the beneficiaries by commercial banks was all pervasive, they need to take suitable action in the matter including strengthening audit of their branches.

The findings of the study suggest that there is a need to reduce the repayment period to 3 years in the case of brick manufacturing units from 7 to 10 years as fixed by most of the banks, since the repayment capacity was higher than the annual debt service liability with three year loan maturity period.

1. This was raised from Rs. 3000 to Rs. 50000 w.e.f. 27.12.90.
2. This was raised from Rs. 5 lakhs to Rs. 10 lakhs w.e.f. 1.3.93.
3. One operating cycle is defined as the interval between the time of procurement of raw materials and that of the realization of sale proceeds of the output.

10

Study of Bank Finance to Small Scale Sector in the Post-Reform Period

Dr. P.C. Misra*

Mr. G.K. Patra**

Introduction

The importance of industrialization as a means of achieving and rapid growth and prosperity has all-along been recognized in the thinking on development strategy for independent India.[1] The Indian economy being a developing one is confronted with the paradox of growth and unemployment in its attempt at industrialization. The most effective way of reducing unemployment is to inculcate the spirit of entrepreneurship among the educated unemployed youths, which will result in chain effect of growth as the successful entrepreneur will continue to expand their activity rapidly.[2] For achieving higher growth rates and maintaining high levels of employment, promoting entrepreneurship through small-scale sector seems to be the most appropriate for the development process.[3] Growth through small industry is advocated due to low investment, higher employment and high value added per one rupee, dispersal of industries and social change. In fact small-scale

* **Reader in the P.G. Department of Commerce, Berhampur University, Berhampur.**

** **Senior Lecturer in the Department of Commerce, Kendrapara College, Kendrapara.**

industries are considered as the instruments of change, growth and diversification.[4] In view of this, an elaborate institutional structure has been created to meet the credit requirement of this sector by embarking on a multi-agency approach. While the Commercial Banks (CBs) provide mainly working capital support, State Financial Corporation (SFC) extends mail term credit to the SSI sector. These apart, Regional Rural Banks (RRBS). District Central Cooperative Banks (DCCBS) and Urban Co-operative Banks (UCBS) also extend credit support to SSIs. At the Apex level, Small Industries Development Bank of India (SIDBI) provides refinance and Co-ordinates the activities of all these agencies engaged in providing assistance to SSIS. In addition, NABARD also provides refinance for extending assistance to the non-farm sector (covering traditional segment of the SSI sector).

Importance of Commercial Banks

Among the various agencies extending credit and facilities to SSIs, the role of Commercial Banks has been quite significant. It has almost monopolized the financing of working capital needs of the small industry sector. It is observed that about 78 per cent of the working capital needs of the SSI sector of our country in the year 1997 has been met by the commercial Banks. Again out of the aggregate funds made available to the SSIs as at the end of March 1997, the share of public sector banks was as high as 74 per cent. The difference of 26 per cent was extended by institutions like SIDBI, RRBs and private and foreign banks.[5]

Despite the increasing role of commercial banks, it is often said that the SSI sector is grossly under financed. A recent estimate of the Expert Committee on Small Enterprises (1997) highlights the widening demand-supply gap in the industrial credit to SSI sector.[6] Since commercial banks are the major source of working capital financier to SSIs it is interesting to examine the role of Commercial Banks in financing the SSI sector.

Objéctives of the Study

The preset study attempts to throw light on the flow of credit to the small-scale sector from the Schedule Commercial Banks (SCBS). In this context a comparison in the trend of SSI financing has been drawn between the all India figures, and that of the figures relating to the state of Orissa, to highlight the position of SSI financing in Orissa, during the post liberalization period.

Period of Study

Ten years data, starting from 1990-91 to 1999-2000 has been compiled from various reports and annual survey of industries of Govt. of Orissa. These years are years relating to the post-liberalization period where the New Economic Policy (NEP) is in operation.

The New Economic Policy

The new economic policy (NEP) with its emphasis of Liberalization, Privatization and Globalization (LPG) has heralded a new phase in the history of small-scale sector having a series of challenges and opportunities. The dismantling of many controls, restrictions, and regulations has opened up opportunities to grow and expand for both the industry and the banking sector. Simultaneously it has also exposed the banks and the small industry to an alien international competitive environment where the only law prevalent is the "*Survival of the fittest*".

Expert Committee Reports: Observations

In order to increase the credit flow to the SSI sector, the GOI and the RBI have appointed at least four committees/Expert Groups. These Committees have made a number of suggestions for making timely and adequate credit to SSI sector for its healthy and orderly growth. For example, in order to ensure adequate and timely flow of institutional credit to SSI, *Shri. P.R. Nayak Committee* (1991) recommended: (i) to give preference to village industries and the tiny units while meeting the credit needs of small scale sectors: (ii) grant working capital limits to SSI units whose credit limit in the individual cases was upto Rs. 50 lakhs (since enhanced to Rs. 4 crores compute on the basis of minimum of 20 per cent of their estimated annual turnover (iii) extend single-widow scheme of SIDBI to all districts of the country; and (iv) to set-up specialized SSI branches where SSI units have been concentrated. An Expert Committee headed by Dr. Adid Hussain on Small Enterprises followed this Committee in 1995. This Committee submitted its reports in January 1997 embodying a set of recommendations for future growth and better performance of small enterprises. According to the Abid Hussain Committee, India needs a new SSI policy framework that is much more promotional than protective; that will develop entrepreneurship; and be much more growth oriented than in the past. *The Informal Group Constituted by the Planning Commission, GOI (Dr. G. Thimmaiah)* also examined bank credit to SSIs so as to make credit delivery system more friendly for borrowers as well as banks; (iii) grievances redressal machinery and miscellaneous issues like marketing of credit facilities, access to technology information, software, corporatisation of SSIs, micro-credit, women entrepreneurs, weaker sections, HRD, etc. At the instance of the Deputy Chairman, Planning Commission, GOI, a Study Group on Development of Small Enterprises was set-up in *May 1999 under the Chairmanship of Dr. D.P. Gupta,* Member of Planning Commission. The Group had made several recommendations relating to legal framework, reservation and other policy issues, definition and scope, infrastructure and human resource development, financial and fiscal measures, and technological and marketing thrust for exports, etc.[7]

SSI Financing by SCBs in India

Table-10.1 exhibits the data pertaining to the advances made by the Schedule Commercial Banks (SCBs) over the period of 10 year our study (1990-91 to 1999-2000) in our country. The following facts can be observed from the table.

Table—10.1 Sectoral deployment of advances of SCBS in the All India level

(Rs. in crores)

Year	*Total advances outstanding*	*Advances outstanding to industrial sector*	*Advances outstanding to SSI*	*C/B X 100*	*C/A X 100*	*B/A X 100*
	(A)	*(B)*	*(C)*			
1	*2*	*3*	*4*	*5*	*6*	*7*
1990-91	124202.93	59093.22	17855.42	30.2	14.38	47.58
1991-92	136705.82	65212.57	16408.63	25.1	12.00	48.05
1992-93	162467.29	78964.34	18263.93	23.12	11.24	48.60

(Table Contd...)

1	2	3	4	5	6	7
1993-94	175891.27	84688.46	19920.01	23.25	11.35	48.15
1994-95	210939.10	96210.93	21721.96	22.5	10.30	45.61
1995-96	254692.11	122259.52	25822.70	21.12	10.13	48.00
1996-97	284373.30	140313.60	26793.32	19.00	09.42	49.34
1997-98	329944.44	161095.94	28628.29	17.70	08.67	48.82
1998-99	382425.03	187946.88	31428.43	16.70	08.21	49.15
1999-2000	460080.68	213778.82	35069.87	16.40	07.62	46.46
Total	2521721.97	1209564.28	241912.56			
Average	252172.2	120956.428	24191.26	21.509	10.332	47.976
C.G.R.	13.99	13.72	6.98			

Source: Compiled from the Banking Statistics (RBI).

(a) The total advance made by the SCBS to various sectors in absolute term amounts to Rs. 252172.97 crores, while the advance to the industrial sector is Rs. 1209564.28 crores. Further the advance to SSI sector is Rs. 241912.56 crores.

(b) The average share of the industrial sector and the small-scale industrial sector in the total advances made by the SCBs are 47.97 and 10.33 per cent respectively.

(c) The average share of the small industrial sector is nearly 21.50 per cent of the advances made to the industrial sector.

(d) On a detail analysis it can be seen that the share of the SSI sector advances has gone down from 30.2 per cent in the year 1990-91 to 16.4 per cent in 1999-2000 in relation to the industrial sector advances. A clear and persistent declining trend is observed in this respect.

(e) A similar declining trend can also be observed in the case of the share of the SSI sector advances in relation to the total advances, where the share of SSIs has gone down from 14.38 per cent in 1990-91 to 07.62 per cent in 1999-2000.

(f) The share of the industrial sector advances to that of the total advances made to various sectors fluctuated within a range of 35.33 to 27.71 per cent. From the year 1990-91 to 1994-95, through the share has fluctuated but the fluctuation is erratic. On the other hand a clear-cut moderate declining trend is observed from the year 1995-96 to 1999-2000.

SSI Financing by SCBs in Orissa

Table-10.2 shows the data relating to the SCBs advances in the state of Orissa over the 10 years of our study period. The table reveals the following facts.

Table—10.2 Sectoral deployment of advances of SCBS in Orissa

(Rs. in crores)

Year	Total advances outstanding (A)	Advances outstanding to industrial sector (B)	Advances outstanding to SSI (C)	C/B X 100	C/A X 100	B/A X 100
1990-91	2003.48	664.14	197.74	29.77	9.8	33.15
1991-92	2246.54	793.62	242.57	30.56	10.7	35.33
1992-93	2506.74	867.32	256.05	29.52	10.2	34.59
1993-94	2574.50	877.80	274.87	31.31	10.6	34.10
1994-95	2949.26	972.92	302.97	31.14	10.2	32.98
1995-96	3511.83	1219.83	337.91	27.7	9.6	34.73
1996-97	3507.81	1117.60	300.73	26.9	8.5	31.86
1997-98	4302.08	1315.80	343.47	26.1	7.9	30.58
1998-99	4582.09	1368.71	357.47	26.1	7.8	29.87
1999-2000	5452.52	1511.08	375.25	24.83	6.8	27.71
Total	33636.85	10708.82	2989.03			
Average	3363.685	1070.882	298.903	28.393	9.21	32.49
C.G.R.	10.53	8.57	6.67			

Source: Compiled from the Banking Statistics (RBI).

A Comparative Analysis

(a) While the small-scale sector on an average shares 10.33 per cent of the total advances made by SCBS to all the sectors in India the same for Orissa is only 9.21 per cent.

(b) The share of the advances made of the small-scale industrial sector from that of the industrial sector while stands at 21.50 per cent on an average in India, the same is 28.39 per cent in the case of Orissa.

(c) The compound growth rate observed in financing the small-scale industries over the period of 10 years of our study while stands at 6.98 for India it is 6.62 for Orissa.

(d) The total finances provided by SCBS over the years to various sectors reached to a level of Rs. 252172.97 crores in India and that is Rs. 33636.85 crores for Orissa. So the share of Orissa is only 1.33 per cent of the total advances.

(e) The advances made to the Industrial sector of Orissa shared only 0.88 per cent of the total advances made to the industrial sector of the country.

(f) The Small Scale Industrial Sector of Orissa fetches only 1.23 per cent of the total advances made to this sector by the SCBs in India.

(g) The per capita Gross output in the industry shown in table-10.3 signifies the fact that the state is industrially backward because Orissa has a share of only 48.86 per cent of the per capita gross output of the national standard.

(h) Graph-1 exhibits the trend of finance provided to small-scale industries in the National level (India) and that of Orissa over the period of ten years of our study.

Table—10.3 A comparative statement of various parameters between India and Orissa

Sl. No.	*Parameter*	*India*	*Orissa*	*(4) As a % to (3)*
	1	*2*	*3*	*4*
1.	No. of SSI units (in lakh) Established during 1990-91 to 1999-2000	14.02	0.267	1.90
2.	Employment created during 1990-91 to 1999-2000	58.4	1.52	2.60
3.	Area (Percentage distribution)	100.00	4.7	–

(Table Contd...)

	1	2	3	4
4.	Population (1991 census) (Percentage distribution)	100.00	3.7	–
5.	Credit deposit ratio as on March 2000	57.1	39.8	–
6.	Per capita gross output in industry in Rs. 1997-98	8659.5	4231.2	48.86

Source: Annual Survey of Industries, 2000-2001.

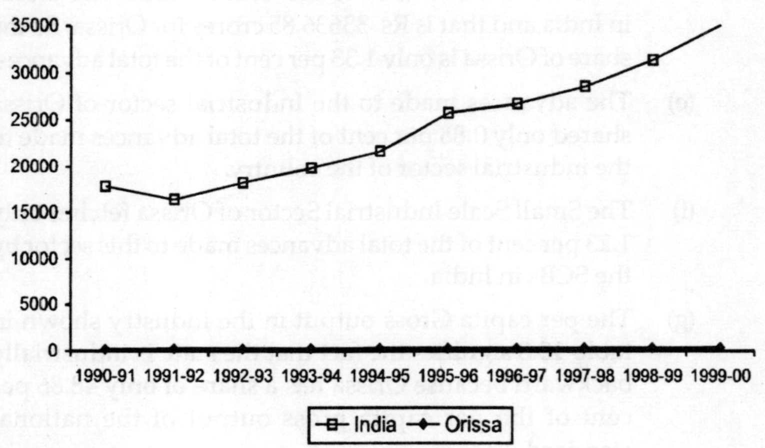

Observations

1. The small scale industries in the national level has a better share of finance from the SCBs (on an average 10.33%) than that of the small-scale industries of the state (on an average 9.21%) of Orissa.

2. In the national level while the SSS fetches 21.50 per cent of the industrial credit advanced by the SCBs, in Orissa SSS fetches 28.39 per cent. This shows that small-scale industries have fetched more of funds from SCBs. It is because Orissa has large number of small-scale industries and it has got a very small number of large-scale industries.

3. On an average Orissa shares only 1.42 per cent of the total advances of the SCBs made in the country over the

period of 10 years of our study. It is really a very meagre amount in comparison to the share of its population, which stands at 3.7 per cent of the nation.

4. Orissa fetches only 0.88 per cent of the advances that were made by the SCBs to the industrial sector of the country. This clearly shows that the state is industrially backward, this is also corroborated by the fact that the per capita gross output in industry in Rupees of the state which is Rs. 4231.2 is far below the national standard of Rs. 8659.5. In fact Orissa's shares is only 48.86 per cent of the national level in the year 1997-98.

5. The small-scale sector of the state has shared only 1.08 per cent from the SCBs advances to the SSIs in the national level. This is not justified on the ground that over the period the number of small-scale those were established in the state has a share of 1.90 per cent of the total industries established in the national level. So the share of advances should have been more.

CHALLENGE AND OPPORTUNITIES

A. For the Small Scale Sector

The challenges facing the SSI sector in the new environment are mainly in the areas of Technology and management. There will be mounting pressure on SSI to upgrade their technology on a continuous basis. The marketing challenges will be more formidable as the small entrepreneurs cannot afford to spend large amount on advertising and sells promotions.[8] As stated earlier, another major challenge will be management. In the new environment, entrepreneurs will have to upgrade their management skills. Areas requiring particular attention are inventory management, costing and financial management. Entrepreneurs will monitor the business environment on a continuous basis.

The service sector, which is expanding at a much faster rate, offers a large-scale opportunities for the small-scale entrepreneurs. Ancillarisation of the SSI sector will pave a way for technology up-gradation and marketing of the SSI products.

B. For the Banking Sector

1. Recognizing the importance of quality products and upgradation of technology as important tools for sustaining SSIs in the competitive market, the banks should encourage the building up of quality culture among the small industries through designing financial assistance schemes and programmes.
2. The mere upgradation of technology alone will not enhance the quality of products in the SSI. There is a need for upgradation of skills of the owners, managers, supervisors and skilled workers. The banks should see that operational skill is upgraded by providing proper training.
3. Banks and other financial institutions should provide Liberal support of financing in the setting up of in-house testing and common testing facilities. The banks and Financial Institutions also have to obtain quality audit of their assisted units.
4. The development of e-commerce (Internet Technology) offers opportunity for low cost marketing mechanism. The role of the banking sector would also need to undergo a change. Banks would therefore have to act, as the business partners of small enterprises by providing them e-commerce facilities and external information required by the small business.

Conclusion

In the emerging environment of competition from within as well as from the imported products, Small-Scale Industrial units will find it more difficult than the larger ones to survive and grow. Even in the earlier protective environment, there have been problems for small entrepreneurs. Despite the fact that the increasing liberalization and globalization of the economy will aggravate some of these problems, there will be new opportunities for small entrepreneurs those who are willing to accept challenges. The experience of many developed and developing countries, including the newly developed high performing Asian Economies suggest that the role of the SSI does not diminish in any with economic liberalization and market orientation.

REFERENCES

1. Ahluwalia I.J. (1998) "Industrial Policy and Industrial Performance in India". Lucase D. Rebert and Paperck. F. Gustav, Ed. *The Indian Economy*, Delhi, Oxford University press.

2. Krishna Kumar, T. "Entrepreneurial Success: An Empirical Study in Mahboob Nagar District" *SEDME (NISET)* Vol. XXV No-3, Sep. 98 p. 29.

3. Reddy K.C. (1988) *Sickness in Small Scale Industry*, Delhi, Ashish.

4. Dawar Ram: "*Financing of Plant and Equipment Acquisition in Small Scale Sector in India*".

5. "Credit to SSIs Doubles to 31,542 Crores". *The Financial Express*, September 1997.

6. Ramesh K. "*Bank Credit to SSI Sector:* A Study in Inter-state Disparity, *Prajnan*, Vol. XXVI, No. 3, 98-99 NIBM, Pune, p. 282.

7. (Dr.) Kulkarni, P.R. Credit flow to SSI during the Post-reform Period *IBA Bulletin*, Vol. XXII No. 11 Nov. 2001

8. Naik, S.D. "Reforms and the SSI sector - II : Challenges and Opportunities" *Business Line* Jan. 16th 1996, p. 6.

11

Financing of Village and Cottage Industries by Regional Rural Banks (RRBs) in Orissa

S.C. Acharya*
A.K. Mohanty**

Nearly 87 per cent of Orissa's population lives in rural areas. The density of rural population in Orissa is the highest in the country. According to the latest estimates of the planning commission (As per the methodology contained in the Report of the Expert Group on Estimation of proportion and Number of poor headed by Lakadawala) Orissa is the poorest state in the country with 47.15 per cent of the population living below poverty line which is much higher than the national average of 26 per cent. The break up of the percentage of people living below poverty line for rural and urban areas are 48.01 per cent and 42.83 per cent respectively. This shows that incidence of poverty is more prevalent in rural areas of the state. These figures are the highest in the country. Nearly 40 per cent of the State's income comes from agriculture. In the absence of adequate irrigation facilities agriculture depends largely on the vagaries of monsoon as a result of which agricultural production fluctuates from year to year. Besides this, 65 per cent of the total

* UGC Teacher Fellow.

** Reader and Head, Department of Commerce, Berhampur University, Orissa.

work force depends directly or indirectly on agriculture for their livelihood. The gap between the per capita income of the State and at the national level was Rs. 316 in 1980-81. This has increased nearly four fold to Rs. 1126 in 1997-98. It is very difficult to bridge this gap in near future in view of the frequent occurrence of natural calamities. The devastation caused by the super cyclone in October 1999 followed by a severe drought situation in 2000 and an unprecedented flood in July 2001 have further compounded the problems of under-development in the state.

The above mentioned socio-economic reasons show that the prime task for the state is removal of poverty and that the key to the development of the State lies in the development of the rural areas. Rural development is a comprehensive programme of activities which encompasses agricultural growth, development of socio-economic infrastructure, provision of gainful employment to the rural poor and removal of poverty. The analysis of performance of the industrial sector in Orissa reveals that village and cottage industries constitute nearly 96 per cent of the total number of industrial units established, only 15 per cent of the total funds investment and 85 per cent of the total employment opportunities created in the industrial sector in Orissa by the end of the year 1999-2000, (Vide Annexure-I). Thus it is evident that village and cottage industries figure prominently in the industrial map of the state. These types of industries with their low capital base have greater employment potential compared to the large and medium scale industries. They play a crucial role in the development of the rural economy of the state. Therefore, this calls for the need to create a more conducive investment climate and to provide incentives and concessions for the promotion of these types of industries in Orissa. This paper deals with the RRBs' financing of Village and Cottage Industries in Orissa. It seeks to ascertain the role of RRBs in the State in terms of

(i) Cumulative disbursement of RRBs' finance to the Village and Cottage Industries in Orissa;

(ii) Annual disbursement of RRBs' loan to this sector in the state; and

(iii) Employment generation by RRBs' through the financing of village and cottage industries in the state.

The study is based on the secondary data compiled from the statistics on RRBs, NABARD publications, Mumbai, Directorate of Handicrafts and Cottage Industries, Bhubaneswar and Directorate of Industries, Orissa, Cuttack. The data cover the period from 1990-91 to 1999-2000. Regional Rural Banks (RRBs). Often known as 'Poor man's bank', were created as per the recommendation of the Working Group on Rural Banks under the Chairmanship of Shri M. Narasimham in 1975. These banks are mandated for the economic upliftment of the rural poor by supplementing the existing banking facilities in rural areas. Their approach to rural credit is sectoral i.e. lending to certain specified categories of customers, viz. small and marginal farmers, landless agricultural labourers, rural artisans and other weaker sections of the rural populations. Providing term loans for promotion of village and cottage industries has been one important agenda of their credit policy. There are 9 RRBs in Orissa established in phases and have been functioning since 1976 with a network of 843 branches as on 31 March 2000. About 764 RRBs branches constituting nearly 91 per cent are operating in rural areas of the State.

The analysis of the performance of the RRBs with regard to their financing of village and cottage industries in Orissa reveals that: The outstanding advances of RRBs in Orissa to this sector have increased from Rs. 16.74 crore in 1990-91 to Rs. 52.40 crore in 1999-2000 registering an overall average growth rate of 12.22 per cent per annum. RRBs' finance to the cottage and Village Industries constitutes nearly 8 per cent of their total outstanding advances during the period under review, (Vide Annexure-II).

Annual disbursement of loan to the sector by RRBs in Orissa constitutes about 25 per cent of the total investment in this sector in the state during the period of study, (Vide Annexure-III). The sharp rise in the RRBs finance to this sector since 1996-98 may be in response to the revised Industrial Policy 1996 of the Govt. of Orissa laying emphasis on improvement of investment climate for the promotion of Village and Cottage Industries in the state.

If the number of RRBs' loan account (under this category) is assumed as an indicator of the number of persons than RRBs' share about 10 per cent of the total number of persons employed in the villages and cottage industries sector in Orissa by providing means of livelihood to nearly 10,000 hands in this sector in different capacities per annum during the period of study, (Vide Annexure-IV).

RRBs by providing term loans to the Village and Cottage Industries for acquisition of productive assets, are contributing directly to certain of assets in rural areas of Orissa. Financing of RRBs to this sector not only helps in income generation and creation of employment opportunities in rural areas of the state but also in augmenting the financial resources of the rural artisans and promoting their age old ancestral professions. RRBs are not mere credit agencies, they are more than that. In fact, they are fruitful exercise in bank led rural growth.

ANNEXURE—I

Performance of the Industrial Sector in Orissa
(By the end of 1999-2000)

Sl. No.	*Type of Industries*	*No. of Units established*	*Investments (Rs. in Lakhs)*	*Employment generation (No. of persons)*
1.	Large and Medium Industries	349 (0.02)	1899.55 (48.60)	82.014 (2.48)
2.	Small Scale Industries	62,264 (4.00)	1423.14 (36.41)	4,14,921 (84.95)
3.	Village and Cottage Industries	14,92,471 (95.98)	586.12 (14.99)	28,04,192 (84.95)
	Total	**15,55,084 (100)**	**3,908.81 (100)**	**33,01,127 (100)**

Note: Figures in brackets indicate percentage to the total.

Source: 1. Directorate of Handicrafts and Cottage Industries, Orissa, Bhubaneswar.

2. Directorate of Industries, Orissa, Cuttack.

ANNEXURE—II

Cumulative Disbursement of RRBs' Finance to Village and Cottage Industries in Orissa (Period from 1990-91 to 1999-2000)

(Rs. in Crore)

Years	*Outstanding advances to village and Cottage Industries*	*Growth (%)*	*Total outstanding advantages of RRBs*
1990-91	16.74 (7.62)	–	219.55
1991-92	18.07 (8.21)	7.95	220.20
1992-93	19.46 (7.94)	7.65	245.20
1993-94	21.97 (8.20)	12.90	267.98
1994-95	24.18 (7.57)	10.06	319.39
1995-96	29.44 (7.55)	21.75	390.08
1996-97	37.53 (8.32)	27.48	451.33
1997-98	45.29 (8.53)	8.53	531.13
1998-99	42.02 (6.73)	6.73	624.01
1999-2000	52.40 (6.88)	6.88	761.71
Average	30.71 (7.61)	12.22	403.06

Note: Figures in brackets indicate percentage to the total.

Source: Statistics on RRBs, NABARD, Mumbai.

ANNEXURE—III

RRBs' Share in Total Investment in Orissa in Village & Cottage Industries (Period from 1990-91 to 1999-2000)

(Rs. in Lakhs)

Sl. No.	*Year (1st April to 31st March)*	*RRBs Loans to Village & Cottage Industries*	*Total Investment (in Orissa) in Village & Cottage Industries*
1	2	3	4
1.	1990-91	132.89 (6.42)	2070.15
2.	1991-92	276.17 (10.32)	2675.67
3.	1992-93	386.74 (14.05)	2751.72
4.	1993-94	389.11 (12.56)	3098.31
5.	1994-95	501.87 (17.59)	2853.66
6.	1995-96	672.26 (18.59)	3616.86

(Contd...)

1	2	3	4
7.	1996-97	1685.84 (42.94)	3925.68
8.	1997-98	2800.19 (57.31)	4886.16
9.	1998-99	2104.40 (35.86)	5869.00
10.	1999-00(P)	1753.69 (29.44)	5956.00
	Average	**924.13 (24.51)**	**3770.44**

Note: Figures in brackets indicate percentage to the total.

Source: 1. Directorate of Handicrafts and Cottage Industries, Orissa, Bhubaneswar.

2. Statistics on RRBs, NABARD, Mumbai.

ANNEXURE—IV

RRBs Share in Total Employment Generation through the Financing of Village & Cottage Industries in Orissa. (1990-91 to 1999-2000)

Sl. No.	*Year (1st April to 31st March)*	*No. of RRBs' Loan accounts to the Village & Cottage Industries*	*Total no. of persons employed in this sector (in Orissa)*	*(3) As percentage of (4)*
1.	1990-91	5986	128218	4.67
2.	1991-92	8196	119788	6.84
3.	1992-93	10123	100506	10.07
4.	1993-94	10802	114527	9.43
5.	1994-95	8883	104185	8.53
6.	1995-96	13147	91484	14.37
7.	1996-97	10049	76516	13.13
8.	1997-98	11939	82941	14.39
9.	1998-99	11707	92822	12.61
10.	1999-00 (P)	7374	94598	7.80
	Average	10249	100679	10.18

Note: (P) Provisional

Source: 1. Statistics on RRBs NABARD Mumbai

2. Economic Survey, Govt. of Orissa (1999-2000).

12

Institutional Financing of Small Scale Industries in Orissa

A Study of OSFC Financing the Village and Tiny Industries

Ch. P.K. Das*

D.K. Mohanty**

Dr. B. Behera***

Transforming Orissa into a vibrant industrial state remains an important goal in the beginning of new millennium. The state being endowed with abundant mineral and forest resources, long coast lines and inland waters, skilled rural artisans and rich cultural heritage, Orissa is poised to be a privileged destination for industrial investment. On the face of fast changing market scenario, the market forces compel large-scale industries to have higher dependence on the small scale industries (SSI) sector. This sector is having a share of more than 40 per cent of the output of the manufacturing sector. Further, total exports of the SSI sector amount for 34.9 per cent of India's total exports and constitutes nearly 35 per cent of the country's industrial workers.

* **Senior Faculty Members, P.N. College, Khurda.**

** **Senior Faculty Members, Nimapara College, Nimapara.**

*** **Senior Faculty Members, Ekmra College, Bhubaneswar.**

Majority families in Orissa belongs to the category of small and marginal farmers, agricultural labourers as well as rural artisans. Thus, financing the village and tiny Industries (V & TI) enjoys a special significance while rural poverty is attributed to unemployment and under-employment. However, various Industrial Policy Resolutions (IPR) of the state have made provisions of incentives to the small V & TIs. The latest IPR, 2001 has emphasized upon the investment opportunities in the SSIs including V & TIs. This IPR has also exempted sales tax on finished product of Khadi, Village, Cottage and Handicraft Industrial Units. Finished product of all existing and new such industrial units are also exempted from sales tax when sold at sales outlets of authorized co-operatives/Govt. agencies and agencies recognized by Khadi and Village Industries Commission/Board, Coir Board, Handicraft Corporation and District Industries Centres (DICs). It has also innovated a new idea, i.e., cluster approach where in SSI, Tiny and Household units will be encouraged in cluster rather than in isolated locations with the involvement of financial institutions, e.g., SIDBI, NABARD and UNIDO Cluster Development and TBIP (Technology Bureau of Industrial Investment partnership).

Objectives of the Study

1. To make a comparison of the quantum of OSFC Financing to the SSI sector with that of the Village and Tiny sector.
2. To study the trend of the OSFC Financing to the V & TIs.
3. To examine the employment generation by the V & TIs Financed by the OSFC.

Scope of the Study and Methodology

The V & TIs for the purpose of the study included Handloom, Powerloom, Khadi and Rural Industries, Tiny units, Handicrafts, Sericulture and Coir Industries in Orissa. The limit of investment in a Tiny Industries has been prescribed to go upto a maximum of Rupees 25 lakhs.

This study is based on the secondary data collected from the annual reports of the OSFC, SIDBI, NABARD, and from the records of the Director of the Handicraft, Cottage Industries, Economic

Survey Reports and various IPRs of Orissa. The present study is confined to a period of 5 years i.e., from the financial year (FY) 1994-95 to 1998-99.

Financing the V & TIs

This section examines the magnitude of investment and the number of SSIs and V & TIs financed by the OSFC (Table-12.1). Since the inception of the OSFCA till the FY ending 31st March 1999 OSFC has financed to the tune of Rs. 89475.13 lakhs to 43,817 SSI units whereas Rs. 2091.97 lakhs to 9317 V & TIs. As evidenced from the table total number of units in V & TIs sector constitutes only 17 per cent of the total units of SSI and village & Tiny Sectors sanctioned up to 31st March'99 and amount of OSFC investment to the sector is only 2.3 per cent of the total investment in SSI sector including the V & TIs.

Table—12.1 Number of Units and Quantum of Investment Since Inception till 31.03.99

	S.S.I. Sector	*V & TIs Sector*
Number of units sanctioned	43817	9317 (17.2)
Investment by OSFC (Rs. in Crores)	89475.13	20.92 (2.3)

Source: The Annual Reports of the OSFC, 1998-99.

Note: Figures in parenthesis is the percentage of V & TIs of the SSIs.

In Table-12.2, it is observed that investment of the OSFC in V & TIs has declined sharply over the period of study. This decline is attributed mainly to the general economic slow down at the national level in the post-liberalization period. This may also be due to the low incentive provided by the State Government as per the IPR 1996. Further, it may be caused due to the fall in exchange rates and inadequate market support by the Government and other agencies. In this table, it is found that in the year 1996-97 there was a significant change in the partner of employment mainly due to the increasing employment in Powerloom and Tiny sectors. However, in the year 1996-97 Powerloom industries have been given priority by the Government.

Table—12.2 OSFC Financing of SSIs vis-à-vis V & TIs

Types of Industries	*1994-95*			*1995-96*			*1996-97*			*1997-98*			*1998-99*		
	No	*Amt.*	*Emp.*	*No*	*Amt.*	*Emp.*	*No*	*Amt.*	*Emp.*	*No*	*Amt.*	*Emp.*	*No*	*Amt.*	*Emp.*
Handloom Industries	–	0.84	22	–	–	–	1	1.52	69	1	0.75	14	–	–	–
Powerloom	1	0.54	6	2	–	8	1	1.31	92	5	6.57	41	–	–	–
Khadi and Rural Industries	–	–	–	–	–	–	–	–	–	–	–	–	–	–	–
Tiny Sector	20	163.13	259	17	25.50	52	10	49.51	389	–	–	–	15	52.16	–
Handicraft	–	7.82	–	–	–	–	–	–	–	–	–	–	–	–	–
Sericulture	–	–	–	–	–	–	–	–	–	–	–	–	–	–	–
Coir Industries	3	5.71	34	2	1.30	18	12	52.34	7	–	–	–	–	–	–
Total	**24**	**178.04**	**321**	**21**	**26.80**	**78**	**24**	**104.68**	**557**	**6**	**7.32**	**55**	**15**	**52.16**	**–**

Source: The Annual Reports, OSFC.

Further, Table-12.3 examines industries-wise cumulative investment and employment generated in V & TI sector till 31.03.99. Investment and employment in sericulture and handicraft industries is found to be insignificant.

Table—12.3 Investment and Employment Generation in V & TI Sector Financed by the OSFC since inception upto 31.03.99

Types of Industries	*Disbursement*		*Employment*
	No	*Amount*	*No*
Handloom Industries	5353	321.86	16059
Power loom	979	513.23	9790
Khadi and Rural Industries	513	10.13	2565
Tiny Sector	1302	854.95	3965
Handicraft	39	7.86	78
Sericulture	13	11.19	39
Coir Industries	21	54.58	105
Total	**8220**	**1773.80**	**32601**

Source: The Annual Reports, OSFC.

Conclusion

The V & TIs in Orissa have not received proper attention of the OSFC to meet their financial requirements. Rural entrepreneurs also fail to obtain adequate finance from the OSFC mainly due to the urban location of the OSFC branches. They normally meet their financial needs from the Co-operative Societies and the Regional Rural Banks (RRBs). Also, various schemes launched by the Government of India such as IRDP, ERRP, PMRY, etc. also provide finance to the V & TIs. In the given perspective, the OSFC needs to harness marketing support and other incentives for the development of SSIs including V & TIs.

REFERENCES

1. *Annual Reports* of the OSFC, SIDBI.
2. *Economic Survey*, Government of Orissa.
3. *Industrial Policy Regulations*, Government of Orissa.
4. Pattnaik K.M. (1996): *Rural Industrialization*.

13

Interplay Between Primary Sector Lending and S.S.I. Development in Orissa

Empirical Evidences from Khurda District

Dr. P.C. Tripathy*

Dr. K.B. Das**

Sri C.R. Panda***

Introduction

Finance is the sine-qua-non of industrialisation. In relation to industrialisation in Orissa, finance is a very crucial factor as then is absolute shortage of investment fund and working capital in the state. Several financial institutions have come forward with special packages of industrial finance under the banner of primary sector lending to encourage rural employment through small and cottage industries.

Indian experience till date indicates that even with high rate of industrial growth, the excess work-force can not be fully employed in the rural areas. So additional employment is to be generated in

* **Senior Professor, P.G. Department of Commerce, Utkal University, Vanivihar.**

** **Senior Lecturer, P.N. College, Khurda.**

*** **Senior Lecturer, P.N. College, Khurda.**

the rural area either through intensification of agriculture or promotion of rural industries. It was surprising to note that there was a continuous decline in the average growth rate in employment, during the period 1972 to 1983 and 1993 to 1998 (Hovered around 1.55 to 2.2 per cent), while the overall economic growth was around 3.5 per cent in agriculture, 7.5 per cent in industry and 7.46 per cent in services during the same period. Hence the panacea to this growing problem can be fond only with the growth of the economy and an employment planning.

It is a fact that the resources in the rural areas are getting transferred to urban areas along with the jobs, which would have been created in rural areas are lost to urban areas. The organised economic sectors are not able to absorb these people, as they do not have any employable skills. Augmenting rural resources (men and material) may be an effective means in generating employment opportunity to the ruralities.

There are three general ways of generating employment in the rural areas. They are

(i) Re-distribution of land or land reforms. This is a Herculean task before the govt. to implement.

(ii) The second option is to check the rate of growth of population. But despite sincere efforts by the government the average annual growth rate of population could be brought down below 2.4 per cent.

(iii) This third option is feasible only with the identification of appropriate projects in the rural areas which should take into account labour intensity, sustainability and capacity to enlarge its production base. That is why, the proliferation of sustainable micro-enterprises in the rural areas has become necessity at this juncture.

Of course, some development observers have viewed that some labour intensive rural industries (like handicrafts) have fallen to the onslaught of larger scale, organised and high-tech urban industries. They have a doubt about the sustainability of these rural industries. But the academicians and researchers have found with evidence that the rural industries or tiny industries sector is dynamic enough to explore new avenues for new products in demand in the market. With the transformation of demand of these products, in various forms, the relevance of small scale rural industries has been gaining importance.

Though a lot of schemes and programmes have been adopted from time to time in order to tap the employment and export potential of the rural small industries, but they could not be popular. Many of these programmes could not be implemented in the spirit with which they were formulated. In addition to this, this sector is subjected to many problems, e.g. uncertainly or unstable demand, increasing opportunity cost of training, lowering of skill and quality and transport costs etc. most of the problems can be solved by providing infrastructure increased resource allocation and well co-ordinated programmes.

Nevertheless credit is one of the crucial inputs for accelerating the process of rural industrialisation and among all infrastructural facilities is a basic component. The major emphasis on policy measures of rural finance has been its progressive institutionalisation to ensure adequate and timely flow of credit to this sector. To cope with the multi-dimensional problems, a multi-agency approach consisting of Commercial Banks, Regional Rural Banks, Co-operative Banks, State Financial Corporation from the financial institutions and Small Industries Development Corporation, Nations Small Industries Corporation, Khadi and Village Industries Commission as Govt. Agencies have been in operation to day. As an incentive to financial institution for providing lending facilities, the Deposit Insurance and Credit Guarantee Corporation , a wholly owned subsidiary of Reserve Bank of India was created. The NABARD has also been established as an apex institution to provide refinance and technical support.

Among different schemes implemented by financial institutions the "Sectoral cum Target Approach" and "Area Approach" were oriented to meet the demands of small industrial in rural areas. Advances to certain sectors were treated, as priority sector advances. The concept of priority sector was evolved to ensure that the assistance from financial institutions flowed in an increasing manner to the sectors, which were declared as national priorities. This concept has been reviewed from time to time by the government and Reserve Bank of India. In 1974, the public sector banks were advised by RBI to channelise at least one-third of their credit to priority sector. During 1979 the banks were again advised to raise the proportion of credit to the priority sector to 40 per cent.

The priority sector includes:

(a) Agriculture (marginal and small farms);

(b) Village Industries (capital requirement not exceeding Rs. 25,000); and

(c) The beneficiaries of IRDP.

Advances to this sector was granted at lower rate of interest in comparison to other advances. From the share of 40 per cent advances allowed to priority sector, it is stipulated that at least 40 per cent of priority sector advances, i.e. 16 per cent of total advances should be channelised to small scale industries. Again this is fragmented into two categories—industries with investment upto Rs. 5 lakhs and industries with investment up to 25 lakhs from Sept. 1998. The special feature of composite Term Loan is that, the repayment period varies between 3 to 10 years basing upon the debt servicing capacity, nature of activity, operating cycle cash generation and borrowers sustenance needs. But at no point of time the loan balance is allowed to exceed the depreciated or resale value of equipments. There is also a moratorium period of 12 to 18 months both on interest and capital. 10 to 20 per cent of the advances are treated as contingency to meet operational bottlenecks or consumption expenditure. It does not require third party gurarantee but only the hypothecation of assets created out of loan.

Small scale industries, tiny sector units, artisanal units, village industries are considered under category of small scale industries of priority sector lending. The definition of small scale industry and ancillary industry has been changed on various accessions by Government and Reserve Bank of India. Based on the recommendation of Abid Hussain Committee, the definition has been revised upward. As per the latest definition, small scale industrial units are those, engaged in the manufacture, processing or presentation of goods and whose investment in plant machinery does not exceed Rs. 3 crores (RBI).

Taking into account the contribution of rural industry to total industrial production (more than 40 per cent), to exports (35 per cent) and generation of employment (154 lakhs, 1981 census), a committee under the Chairmanship of the then Deputy Governor of Reserve Bank of India, Sri P.R. Nayak was constituted in December 1991 to look into the flow of credit from banks to this sector. The findings of the committee revealed that the small scale industries sector received working capital from banks only to the extent of 8.1 per cent of the value of their outputs and tiny and village industries share was only 2.7 per cent. On the recommendation of this committee, priority had to be given to the village industries and other small scale industrial units in the order.

The Present Study

The above mentioned policies can be properly implemented, if they are based on the knowledge of the real world situation regarding the availability of credit nature and extent of utilisation and their impact on SSI development. It is with this objective in mind the present study is planned to highlight the linkage between finance and industrialisation with the help of data collected from sample industrial units.

The objectives set up for this study are:

— To evaluate the role of financial institutions in promoting rural industries through priority sector advances,

— To determine the problems and prospects of small scale units and to examine the impact of institutional finance on the viability of rural industries.

This research paper has been prepared with the help of both secondary and primary data. The required secondary data were collected from reports and publications of various government departments and financial institutions responsible for small scale industries promotion. The required primary data for this study was collected through field survey during 1997-98 in Khurda district. It was considered desirable to select villages on the basis of institutional assistance provided to each village by commercial Banks for development of rural small scale industries. Loan intensity during the year 1996-98 was taken as the major factor for inclusion of villages. Thus a total of 55 villages were selected for the purpose of field study.

In consultation with the financing agencies, it was ascertained that small scale entrepreneurs in the following industry type were financially assisted.

Category I	Cashew processing units, Rice Mills and Paddy Processing Units (Agro-produce processing units)	12 + 24 = 36	8 + 16 = 24	66.66
Category II	Coir and Carpet + wood carving and wooden toys + Bamboo and Cane works	26 + 15 + 8 = 49	12 + 8 + 3 = 23	46.93
Category III	Appliqué works + Terracotta + Pattachitra and Mask making. (Traditional, aesthetic and artistic units)	48 + 16 + 14 = 78	24 + 8 + 8 = 48	52.25
Category IV	Brass and Bell metal + Agril. Implements + Stone carvomgs. (metal and stone units)	56 + 18 + 31 = 105	24 + 10 + 15 = 49	46.61
	Total	268	136	50.74

In this study, two types of ratio analysis based on income statement and balance sheet were applied to assess the risk bearing ability/credit carrying ability of the borrower entrepreneurs.

Income Statement Ratios

(a) $$\text{Operating Ratio} = \frac{\text{Total Operating Expenses}}{\text{Gross Income}}$$

(b) $$\text{Rate of Return on Capital} = \frac{\text{Net Income}}{\text{Total Capital Investment}}$$

Operating ratio less than one and higher rate of return on capital indicates that the borrowed loan generates additional income, which confirms the first R (return from investment of credit).

Balance Sheet Ratios

(a) $$\text{Current Ratio} = \frac{\text{Total Current Assets}}{\text{Total Current Liabilities}}$$

(b) Net Capital Ratio = $\frac{\text{Total Assets}}{\text{Total Liabilities}}$

(c) Average Ratio = $\frac{\text{Total Liabilities}}{\text{Net worth}}$

The above ratios show the current, intermediate and long term liquidity position of the business. Higher ratio (greater than one) indicate adequate risk bearing ability / credit carrying ability of the borrower.

(d) Equity of Asset value Ratio = $\frac{\text{Net Worth}}{\text{Value of Assets}}$

This ratio was used to highlight the overall financial position of the business after availing financial assistance.

To collect accurate data and information directly from individual units efforts were made and all care were taken to elicit correct information from the respondents. A few respondents did not have detailed account books and were speaking from their memory. Some errors might have been caused by partial memory lapses.

Major Findings

This research is undertaken with the primary objective of determining the role played by financial institutions functioning in Khurda district of Orissa in connection with the promotion of S.S.I. units in rural areas as per the guidelines of the RBI. The performances of the financial institutions in this regard in the district over a brief period of five years (1995-96 through 1999-2000) have been presented and analysed in terms of table-13.1 appended to this chapter.

Financial institutions operating in the district have performed very well to supersede the target fixed for priority sector advances for the year 1995-96 (169.53% achievement). But the target fixed for the small scale sector was only 23.42 per unit of priority sector advances during the same year. The guideline prescribed by the Reserve Bank of India to allocate 40 per cent of priority sector credit to S.S.I. sector was flouted. In the case of Co-operative banks it was alarmingly low (6.84 per cent) followed by RRBs 10.42 per cent and Commercial Banks 22.40 per cent. The Commercial Banks have played a commendable role in making credit available to SSI sector (181%) achievement. The overall performances of development of credit to S.S.I. sector in the district was impressive which stand at 159.73 per cent of the target. During the five years beginning with the financial year 1995-96, the same trend was maintained. With the inception of the year 1996-97, the financial institutions allocated less funds to SSI sector than the limit prescribed by the RBI. It was 22.15% of priority sector quota in the year 1997-98, 10.4% in 1998-99 and 21.54% of during 1999-2000. During these five years the lowest allocation to the S.S.I. was made by Co-operative banks which stand at 0.55% of total priority sector advances made by them. However, the OSFC has made a good job by providing 92.19% of its investment funds to S.S.I. sector. Another important aspect of this study is the variations in the provisions for credit to S.S.I. sector during the period of observation. While it was the lowest with 63.27% during 1997-98, the highest was marked during 1999-2000 with 295.34%. An in-depth study of the data presented, revealed that the financial institutions have superseded the target fixed for credit deployment to S.S.I. sector. One reason for such high performance is the fixation of a lower target without assessing the ground realities and marked violation of the prescribed norms.

The reasons attributed by the financial institutions are summarized as follows.

(a) Non-availability of refinance facility from NABARD, as the refinance facility is tied-up with the recovery performance;

(b) Lack of forward and backward linkages between source and application of funds;

(c) Sponsoring of less number of applications by promoting agencies; and

(d) Shifting of emphasis of DRDA in favour of primary and tertiary sector.

Financial Assistance

It is interesting to note in terms of the data provided in the table that the institutional finance has outweighed the non-institutional and other sources of finance. The borrowing from the Commercial banks was Rs. 173354.50, the least observed in case of Category IV industries and Rs. 25251.00, the highest calculated for Category I industries. Whereas except the contribution from their own fund, the borrowing from other sources was very minimum. An inverse relationship was established between these two sources of finance after the extension of financial support. Even though the finance provided by Commercial Banks was adequate enough as was observed from the tables-13.2 and 13.3 (which hovered around Rs. 18000.00) still it couldn't discourage the dependence of SSIs on village moneylenders, creditors, friends and relatives. It was disclosed from the information presented in the table that in case of all the four categories of industries of dependence on non-institutional and other sources may be attributed to the fact that these sources are available at the door-step and at the call and notice of the entrepreneurs on the other hand, on the other hand, to meet the short-term and immediate requirement the entrepreneurs avail it for themselves. Hence, to reduce the importance of the traditional sources, the financial institutions have to be very liberal and pragmatic in their lending policies. Steps should be taken to avoid the undue delay in actual disbursement of finance.

Factual evidence in regard to repayment position revealed that in case of institutions finance, it was at the lower side of 19.52 per cent for category I, 21.55 per cent for category, II 17.86 per cent for category, III and 19.35 per scent for category IV industries. On the same analogy, the corresponding recovery position of the moneylenders and trade creditors was in sharp contrast to the trend noticed in case of Commercial Banks, which on an average constituted more than 80 per cent in case of all the four categories of industries. As such, the magnitude of loan outstanding after two years of finance (as it was ascertained) assumed a staggering proportion of 61 per cent or more in case of the institutional finance and 20 per cent in case of moneylenders and trade creditors. On the basis of the above findings all that can be said is that because of united efforts and personal contacts that led to the higher percentage of recovery by the agencies or sources of finance other than the Commercial Banks.

Capital Investment

Table-13.4 presents the information about fixed capital and working capital of sample industries. The finances obtained have been classified as fixed capital and working capital. Land and Building, Machineries, tools and equipments etc. comprises fixed capital. The sample rural industries have invested quite a substantial amount in fixed capital. As was found from the study, Category I industries which consists of cashew processing plants, rice hanlers etc. accounted for the highest amount of fixed capital (Rs. 67165.70) among the four categories of rural enterprises followed by Category II (Rs. 43835.75), Category III (Rs. 34727.15) and Rs. 31978.43 by Category IV industries. The ratio of fixed capital to total capital was found to be highest in case of Category I industries (72.61 per cent) and the lowest was calculated for Category IV industries (57.13 per cent). So far as the individual item of fixed capital was concerned the land and building contributed maximum percentage (more than 50 per cent on an average). The next important item of fixed capital, i.e. machines and plant accounted for the second expensive component. But a little per cent was spent for tools and equipments by all the categories of industries. However, this little improvement in possession of modern tools and equipments was marked during post-finance period. Factual evidence in regard to working capital is presented in table 3 shows that the sample rural enterprises on an average invested adequate working capital (34.30 per cent) Percentage-wise it was highest in case of category IV industries (42.87 per cent of total capital) and lowest of 27.39 per cent calculated for Category I industries. But in terms of amount, it was Category I industries which spent more on working capital (Rs. 25341.15) and Rs. 21489.70 least amount spent by Category III industries.

A substantial amount of working capital was spent on operating expenses like salary and wages. But almost all the units were found to have invested more than 50 per cent of their working capital in stocks (either raw materials or finished stock). The percentage of credit sale (hovered around 20 per cent) also plays a vital role in the constitution of working capital the proportion of looking capital required to meet the day to day operational expenses was found to be 9 per cent of the working capital on an average at the maximum. It is further evident from the table-13.4 that average capital invested per rural industrial units found to be Rs.67,726.43 during post-finance period. However, it was learnt from the rural entrepreneurs that there was real difficulty in obtaining loan capital as per their requirements. Besides the problem of managing the borrowed capital effectively was also a problem on the part of the entrepreneurs.

Cost-Effectiveness of Industrial Units

Cost-effectiveness is very important for the viability of SSI units in rural areas. These industries usually serve the local markets. So they face demand constraints on the one hand and a perceived lack price by the customer on the other hand. In these circumstances, surplus over cost (operating expenses) earned by a rural industrial promoter is governed by cost of production. Lower is the cost of production, higher is the surplus. It is also a fact that cost-effectiveness assumes importance, as the rural manufacturers can not manoeuvre accounts for the reduction of cost. Hence, an investigation into the structure of cost is required to examine cost-effectiveness and find out ways for increasing the profitability and viability for faster and smother growth of small rural industries. The different composition of total cost incurred by rural industrial units includes cost of (a) raw materials, (b) wages and salaries (c) electricity and fuel, (d) repair and maintenance, (e) depreciation (f) transport (g) rent and taxes, (h) insurance and (i) other miscellaneous expenses.

A bird's eye view of the data contained in table-13.5 brought out the fact that in all the four categories of industries the value added by the manufacturers hovered around 15 to 18 per cent of gross value of production of industries. Accordingly, the return after deduction of interest also averaged between 16 to 20.5 per cent of total operational expenses. Category II industries which consists of industries of aesthetic and artistic goods toped with 20.41 per cent return on operational expenses or working capital investment for a month. It was followed by Category II group of industries with 20.18 per cent and Category I industries earned the lowest per cent of 16.51 per cent on monthly investment of working capital of Rs. 22370.85. In between remained Category IV industries with 17-95 per cent return.

While looking at cost composition it was found that except Category III and IV group of industries, the lion's share of cost was consisted by raw material cost. In category I, the raw material cost was 62.07 per cent of total operational expenses and it was found to be the highest among the four. But the same raw materials demanded only 41 per cent of the monthly working capital in case of Category IV industries. The next major constituent of cost was labour or wages and salaries. The labour cost dominated the cost structure of category III industries with 48.13 per cent of total operational expenses while the same was calculated at 12.13 per cent in case of Category I industries. On the basis of the above observations it can be said that the cost can be reduced by two ways to maximise the surplus; (a) by improvement in the efficiency of the management and effective fund management, and (b) by improving the mode of production through the application of improved technology. A little improvement in the volume of working capital and its effective application could bring in remunerative return to the rural entrepreneurs.

Other Financial Indicators

a. Assets formation

The value of productive and unproductive (consumer durables) assets determines the status of a household in the society and strengthen the risk bearing ability of the entrepreneurs to attract the new investment opportunity in the rural areas. So, it is necessary to examine the asset position of the sample entrepreneurs, who availed of the financial support. A perusal of the data presented in the table-13.6 shows that Category I industries could mobilise the highest asset possession of Rs.106694.18 among the four categories of industries followed by Category II, Category III and the lowest of Rs.64541.61 calculated for Category IV industries. A major chunk of the asset composition was shared by land and workshop building in case of all the categories of industries, next only to the investment made in firm machines and plants. One most important observation of the data presented in the table was that, all the sample enterprises maintained good stock level. The stock included the raw materials, work-in-progress and finished goods. There was also a significant inclusion of financial assets in the composition of assets which plays a very vital role so far as liquidity during exigency is concerned. All these things could be possible due to availability of finance.

Table-13.6 presents a detailed account of the accumulation of assets by the four categories of rural industries. By going through the data it is revealed that depending upon the nature of credit and purpose for which it was sanctioned the composition of long-term and current assets appeared to be conspicuous, in absolute terms as well as in percentage terms. As it is apparent from the estimates, the long-term assets accounted for a lion's share in the constitution of total assets. The long-term assets were found to be only 49.57 per cent in case of category III industries and maximum of 62.00 per cent in case of category I industries. But the real impact of financial assistance can be assessed from the composition of current assets in the total asset structure of the borrower entrepreneurs. The highest percentage of current assets was marked in category III industries and the lowest of 26.94 percent was observed in case of category I industries. The composition of current assets which denotes working capital of the enterprise gives an impressive and boosting trend to the business of rural - industries.

b. Liabilities

In the present study credit disbursed to industrial units constituted the liabilities of the business with provision to make adjustment of subsidy component (if any) and interest due thereon. Logically, these liabilities should be converted into assets in due course. In addition to the loan sanctioned by financial institutions, the non-financial institutions also provide some short-term loans that add to the liabilities of the borrowing entrepreneurs. Usually the tendency of these borrowers was to invest a limited portion of these loans for business purpose and the remaining part was spent on conspicuous consumption. Table-13.7 presents the information on the liability position of the sample borrowers of different categories of rural industries. A glimpse at the information presented in the table revealed that irrespective of the categories of rural industries, intermediate liability constituted the lion's share of total liabilities. An in-depth study of the liabilities depicted that, category III industries owned the highest per cent of intermediate liability (90.02 per cent of the total liability) and category II owned the lowest with 72.08 per cent intermediate liability. In the absence of long-term finance from any quarter, long-term liabilities was virtually absent in case of all the categories of enterprises. The finance provided by the financial institutions was purely meant for an intermediate period which was to be paid back with 10 years from the date of disbursement. As a result of institutional financing, the dominance of current liabilities which prevailed during pre-finance period made its departure.

c. Net-worth

An analysis of change in the level of assets and liabilities of the borrower entrepreneurs provides information regarding owner's equity or net-worth. As it could be seen from the data presented in table13.8 the magnitude of net-worth of the entrepreneurs was highest in case of Category I industries with Rs.71,037.33 and lowest in case of category IV industries with Rs.40821.48.

Ratio Analysis

After determining the balance-sheet and owner's equity of different categories of borrowing entrepreneurs it is necessary to find out the financial performances of industrial units through ratio analysis. The financial ratios based on income statement reveal that the borrowed loan has generated adequate additional return to the entrepreneurs which further confirms by calculating the soundness of credit through return from investment ratio. Less than one operating ratio and higher rate of return on capital indicate that the borrowed loan generated additional income. Higher ratio (greater than one) after bank finance indicate the adequate risk-bearing ability or credit carrying ability or credit worthiness of the borrower. The ratio of equity to value of assets was used to examine the overall financial position of business. The higher values of financial ratios based on balance-sheet, reflect that with the institutional credit, the borrowers have increased adequate risk bearing capability.

The worded out ratios presented in table13.9 revealed the magnitude of operating ratios (a measure for determining whether costs are higher or lower) indicates the proportion of gross income used to meet the operating expenses of an enterprise. This ratio, therefore, helps in comparison of resources use on the one hand and generation of additional income on the other. Viewed from this angle, a close look at the operating ratio estimates presented in the table shows that irrespective of categories of industries, it was less than unity. This was an indication of productive use of borrowed capital in different rural enterprises, which in turn generated additional income.

Rate of return on capital (the ratio of net-income to total capital investment excluding imputed value of family labour) measures the credit worthiness of the entrepreneurs. Higher the magnitude of the ratio, greater is the credit carrying ability and vice-versa. Keeping this aspect in view, a perusal of the ratios worked out for the sample enterprises unveiled not so a satisfactory performance.

The financial ratios provided in table13.9 does not reveal an encouraging indicator for additional investment in sample industries. This could be attributed to the fact that in such labour intensive small scale and cottage industries the net returns failed to commensurate with the level of investment made, specially in costly raw-materials and skilled labour. That is the reason, that irrespective of categories of rural industries, the rate of return was not worth-mentioning as was anticipated to accelerate the living standards of the entrepreneurs and help generate accumulated of assets. Under the existing condition the crying need, therefore, lies in increasing the productivity of each enterprise through modernisation, rendering expertise service in management and market support to ensure a stable flow of income.

The current ratios which measure the degree of financial safety in the short run were in favour of all the sample enterprise after the extension of financial support. This indicates their solvency position to meet the short-term financial obligations. The current ratios worked out for all categories of enterprises were more than unity. It was estimated at 2,88, the lowest in case of Category II industries whereas the highest of 10.918 found for Category III industries.

Leverage ratio or the debt / equity ratios were very much favourable to enterprises after effective utilisation of credit. As it is supported by empirical evidence, the leverage ratio was the lowest 0.451 found in case of Category III industries and the highest. 0.581 calculated or Category IV industries. Hence, it can be said that, the financed industries were more solvent and the financial institutions should not be worried as there is the less amount of risk involved in the realisation of borrowed funds.

The worked out net capital ratio or ratio of total assets to total liabilities, which measures the overall financial strength and solvency position of the industry was highest 3.215 in case of Category III industries and 2.720 the lowest in case of Category IV industries. It was apparent from the information that after the extension of financial assistance the liabilities of the entrepreneurs mounted rapidly and as a result a reduced net capital ratio was found but it was not discouraging.

The conclusion that can be drawn out of the above findings may be summed-up as follows. That the bank finance has made a modest beginning in giving a new lease of life to the rural industries, who in shortest period of time could generate some productive assets that the rural lending institutions often pursue objectives which are considerably different from the objectives adopted by formal lending institutions. The viability of the financial institutions should also be evaluated simultaneously with the evaluation of the credit deployment. The gap that is created in their objectives, speaks, why rural banks have often collapsed while at the sometime aiming that their activities have helped in rural development.

Conclusion

This study has been pursued with the basic objective of determining the interface between primary-sector lending and SSI development in the rural areas several financial institutions including Orissa State Financial Corporation and Co-operative Banks are functioning as the catalysts to provide finance to rural small-scale industries. The NABARD is the apex financial institution which provides refinance to the institutions promotions rural industries. This study pertains to sample SSI units in Khurda district and uses primary data collected through field survey. In addition, secondary data for a period of five years, i.e. 1995-96 through 1999-2000 are also collected and analysed. It is interesting to note that the financial institutions; particularly, the Commercial Banks and the OSFC have done a commendable job to promote SSI units in rural areas of Orissa. Although the RRBS and Co-operative Banks have extended financial support, their performances are not commensurate to the expectations pinned on them. The major findings of the study are summarised below.

A. There has been a perceptible transformation in the social and economic environment within which the village industries are functioning. These industries have open-out basic employment opportunities in the rural areas. An interface between agriculture and industrialisation is visualised through both forward and backward linkages between them. The sample entrepreneurs have become conscious about the availability of liberal finance from the institutional measures provided by financial institutions.

B. It is seen that the guideline provided by the RBI is not followed in some cases. Under primary-sector lending, the financial institutions have not provided finance to SSI units as per the direction of the RBI. This is an area in which improvement is required.

C. The sample entrepreneurs have borrowed substantial portion of their required finance from unorganised sources like moneylenders, friends and relatives. As the rate of interest from these sources are very high, the SSI units have paid high interest on their borrowings. Hence, the financial institutions should come out with more liberal schemes of assistance.

D. In addition of finance, there is need for some promotional measures like marketing assistance, project feasibility report, consultancy and engineering design services. It is suggested that the financial institutions should come-out with these measures for prompt solution of the problems of SSI units.

E. In this study, it is observed that the financial institutions could not provide required funds to the SSI units in required quantity due to non-availability of refinance from the NABARD. The apex organisation for rural development should abandon this practice and come forward with a helping hand to support SSI units in a backward state like Orissa.

F. Direct financing to the rural entrepreneurs by the institutions should be dispensed with. The modus of financing these enterprises should be indirect, that is through the service of Panchayat Raj institution and NGOs. Direct financing has been mainly responsible for a very high percentage of default.

G. "Cash Credit" facility should be extended to the rural entrepreneurs, which should be in the nature of "Working Fund". Under this system, the entrepreneur would be required to retain the working capital resources so long as they maintain a prescribed production level. If there is a fall in the production level, the entrepreneur has to refund the surplus working capital. If the production increases, he would be allowed to get additional working capital from the banks. It means, the working capital finance should be pro-rata to the level of production by the enterprise.

H. In addition, steps should be taken to create more industrial infrastructure in the rural areas. The state should come forward with pragmatic policy measures. Lastly, entrepreneurship development programmes (EDPs) should be conducted for promotion of rural entrepreneurship.

Table—13.1 Plan and Performance of Financial Institutions of Khurda District (1995-1996 to 1999-2000) (Ref. To S.S.I. Sector)

Banks	*Priority Sector*			*S.S.I. Sector*			
	Target	*Achieve*	*% to Achieve*	*Target*	*ACA*	*% to P.S.*	*% of Achieve*
				1995-96			
Com. Banks	224075	510191	227.68	5186	90876	22.40	181.0
RRBs	28695	33351	116.23	2992	2865	10.42	95.75
Co-op.	101175	84555	83.57	6930	28828	92.19	74.65
OSFC	33166	28160	84.91	30578	2828	92.19	74.65
Total	**387111**	**656257**	**169.53**	**90686**	**144851**	**23.42**	**159.73**

(Table Contd...)

			1996-97				
Com. Banks	562107	45501	80.95	222416	122227	39.56	54.95
RRBs	76656	65858	85.91	5106	2029	6.66	39.74
Co-op.	135077	130496	96.61	23250	52264	17.21	224.79
OSFC	132000	107769	81.64	118700	96337	89.92	81.33
Total	**905840**	**759124**	**83.80**	**369472**	**273057**	**40.78**	**73.90**
			1997-98				
Com. Banks	416588	412875	99.10	130851	68797	31.41	52.58
RRBs	113679	65459	57.56	6680	3372	5.88	50.48
Co-op.	182420	84541	46.34	23200	28332	12.72	122.12
OSFC	13037	7844	18.23	6637	5409	15.42	81.50
Total	**755724**	**870719**	**75.51**	**167368**	**105910**	**22.15**	**63.27**
			1998-99				
Com. Banks	496656	433689	87.32	154.52	72305	3.11	467.93
RRBs	195384	107202	54.87	9130	6677	4.67	73.13
Co-op.	182820	128709	70.40	23200	32214	12.69	138.85
OSFC	88800	24	0.02	52400	21	59.00	0.04
Total	**963660**	**669624**	**68.49**	**100182**	**111217**	**10.40**	**90.07**
			1999-00				
Com. Banks	617312	676092	109.62	204199	124591	33.08	61.01
RRBs	208585	151850	72.80	14450	7370	6.93	51.00
Co-op.	253399	189691	74.87	1400	36553	0.55	2610.92
OSFC	589800	590806	987.96	25400	556408	42.47	2190.58
Total	**1139036**	**1609039**	**141.26**	**245449**	**724922**	**21.54**	**295.34**

Table—13.2 Repayment of Borrowed Money

	Sources of Finance	*Category I*	*Category II*	*Category III*	*Category IV*
1.	**Commercial Banks**				
a.	Amount Borrowed	25251.00	18353.00	18271.00	17354.00
b.	Amount Repaid	4928.99	3277.84	3973.40	3357.99
c.	Percentage of Repayment to total	19.52	17.86	21.55	19.35

(Contd...)

2. Other F.I.S.				
a. Amount Borrowed	1267.67	1397.04	1083.35	1120.45
b. Amount Repaid	461.69	717.10	586.20	484.59
c. Percentage of Repayment to total	36.42	51.33	54.11	43.25
3. Money-lenders				
a. Amount Borrowed	6738.63	5417.85	1100.40	3867.92
b. Amount Repaid	5556.00	4259.51	1004.23	2996.09
c. Percentage of Repayment to total	82.45	78.62	91.26	77.46
4. Friends and Relatives				
a. Amount Borrowed	2389.55	2116.22	1046.00	1377.26
b. Amount Repaid	1614.38	1519.86	696.33	1090.24
c. Percentage of Repayment to total	67.56	71.82	66.57	79.16

Table—13.3 Category wise Source wise Distribution of Capital

	Category I	*Category II*	*Category III*	*Category IV*
Own funds	17850.00	10225.20	7215.20	7255.30
Co-operative Banks	25251.00	18353.00	18271.90	17354.50
Other Financial Institutions	1277.67	1094.33	1083.35	1120.45
State Govt. Agencies	0.00	0.00	0.00	0.00
Money Lenders	6738.63	5417.85	1700.40	3867.92
Friends and Relatives	2389.55	2116.22	1046.00	1377.26
Total	**53506.85**	**37206.60**	**28716.85**	**30975.43**

(Capital excluding land and building)

Table—13.4 Category wise Distribution of Fixed and Working Capital per Enterprise

Categories	*No. of units*	*Fixed capital*	*Working capital*	*Total capital*	*Ratio of Ficp*	*Ratio of Working Capital*
Category I	24	67165.70	25341.15	92506.85	72.61	27.39
Category II	23	43835.75	22370.85	66206.60	66.21	33.79
Category III	40	34727.15	21489.70	56216.85	61.77	38.23
Category IV	49	31978.43	23997.00	55975.43	57.13	42.87
Total	**136**	**177707.03**	**93198.70**	**270905.73**	**65.70**	**34.30**

(Contd...)

Average Capital Structure of Sample Units (Fixed Capital)

Categories	*Land and Building*	*Machines*	*Tools and equipments*	*Others*	*Total*
Category I	15222+24000	24575	2570.70	1020.00	67165.70
Category II	12000+17000	11750	2620.40	465.35	43835.75
Category III	11500+16000	5890	882.55	454.60	34727.15
Category IV	12000+13000	5435	1022.18	521.25	31978.43
Total	**50500+70000**	**47650**	**7095.03**	**2461.20**	**177707.03**

Table—13.5 Cost-wise Distribution of Operational Expenses of Financed Rural Industries

Items		*Category I*	*Category II*	*Category III*	*Category IV*
1.	**Gross value of production**	30047.00	27135.66	26120.73	28606.82
2.	**Total Operational Exp.**	25341.15	22370.85	21489.70	23997.10
a.	Raw materials	145728.28 (62.07)	11711.14 (52.35)	9702.59 (45.14)	9839.77 (41.00)
b.	Wages and Salaries	3075.60 (12.13)	6744.81 (30.15)	10342.29 (48.13)	10441.09 (43.51)
c.	Electricity Fuel etc.	1750.00	235.00	185.35	310.00
d.	Repair and maintenance	1414.95	441.75	188.50	292.60
e.	Depreciation	886.80	507.20	277.42	245.72
f.	Transport	915.35	1302.95	465.55	1976.35
g.	Rent and Taxes	506.00	215.00	155.10	521.40
h.	Insurances	527.55	220.00	101.10	175.20
i.	Other Exp.	536.62	993.30	56.50	195.87
	Value added				
3.	**Net value of prod. (Net Returns) by Manufacturers**	4705.85 (15.66%)	4764.81 (17.56%)	4631.03 (17.73%)	4609.82 (16.11%)
4.	**Less Interest**	520.41	249.39	245.35	301.30
5.	**Net Return**	4185.44 (16.51)	4515.42 (20.18)	4385.68 (20.41)	4308.52 (17.95)

(Re-cycling period - 1 month).

Table—13.6 Average Asset Position per Enterprise

Assets	*Category I*	*Category II*	*Category III*	*Category IV*
1. Land and Building (Excluding domicile)	2400 + 15000	17000 + 12000	16000 + 11500	13000 + 12000
2. Livestock	1712.75	1108.151	2000.17	979.30
3. Firm machineries	24575	11750.00	5890.10	5435.00
4. Tools and equipments	2570.70	2620.40	882.55	1022.18
5. Farm Assets	3590.20	1329.85	1885.12	2058.72
6. Non-Agriculture Assets	618.33	771.18	621.75	1271.36
7. Household durables	5882.70	6729.10	6921.55	6518.42
8. Stock (W.I.P.+E.S.T.+R.M.)	12000.00	8560.00	8750.00	8500.00
9. Financial Assets (Deposits + gold, silver + shares etc.)	15724.50	12739.20	14230.55	12235.38
10. Other Assets	1020.00	465.35	454.60	521.25
Total	**106694.18**	**750732.23**	**69136.29**	**64541.61**
Current Assets	28744.50 (26.94)	21764.55 (28.99)	23435.15 (33.90)	21256.63 (32.93)
Intermediate Assets	11803.98 (11.06)	9938.28 (13.24)	11428.59 (16.53)	10827.80 (16.78)
Long term Assets	56145.70 (62.00)	43370.40 (57.77)	34272.59 (49.57)	31457.18 (50.29)
	106694.18 (100.00)	75072.23 (100.00)	69136.29 (100.00)	64541.61 (100.00)

Current Asset = Financial Asset + Stock + Other Assets

Intermediate Assets = Non-Agriculture Assets + Livestock + Household goods + Farm Assets.

Long-term Assets = Land and Building + Firm machineries + Tools and Equipments.

Table—13.7 Category wise Liabilities of Financed Units

	Types of Liabilities	*Category I*	*Category II*	*Category III*	*Category IV*
a.	Current	9128.18	7534.07	2146.40	5245.18
b.	Intermediate	26528.67 (74.40)	19447.33 (72.08)	19355.25 (90.02)	18474.95 (77.89)
c.	Long-term	–	–	–	–
	Total	**35656.85** **(100.00)**	**26981.40** **(100.00)**	**21501.65** **(100.00)**	**23720.13** **(100.00)**

Current liability = Friend and Relatives + Creditors/moneylenders

Intermediate = Commercial Banks + Other F.I.S.

Table—13.8 Net worth of the Financed Units

Particulars	*Assets*	*Liabilities*	*Net worth*
Category I	106694.18	35656.85	71037.33
Category II	75073.23	26981.40	48091.83
Category III	69136.29	21501.65	47634.64
Category IV	64541.61	23720.13	40821.48

Table—13.9 Ratio Analysis

	Category I	*Category II*	*Category III*	*Category IV*
Operating ratio	0.843	0.824	0.822	0.838
Rate of Return on Capital	0.087	0.128	0.161	0.148
Current Ratio	3.148	2.888	10.918	4.052
Leverage Ratio (Debt/Equity)	0.501	0.561	0.451	0.581
Net Capital Ratio	2.992	2.782	3.215	2.720
Equity to Asset Value Ratio	0.665	0.640	0.688	0.632

14

Institutional Financing for Small Scale Industrial Development of Orissa

Dr. Kshirod Kumar Behera*

Introduction

Industrial units are generally classified as small-scale, medium-scale and large-scale considering their size, capital resource and number of labours engaged upon. Generally small-scale industry is located in urban areas. It produces goods with mechanised as well as manual ways.

In India, first industrial policy resolution was adopted on April 06, 1948. Under this resolution, small-scale industries had been included and special emphasis was laid on development of such units. Again another industrial policy resolution was adopted on 30th April 1956, which empowered the state Govt. to continue small industries by restricting the volume of production in the large-scale production and allowing subsidies. In 1977, once again attention had been paid in relation to capital limitation of small-scale industries that the amount of capital was raised to 10 lakhs from 5 lakhs. Again fixed capital investment, a limit was raised to Rs.15 lakhs in 1985, such investment limit was further raised to Rs.35 lakhs by Govt. of India. Further, the industrial policy

* Lecturer, Kharasrota Mahavidyalaya, Singhpur, Dt. Jajpur, Orissa.

resolution, 1990 raised ceiling in plant and machinery to Rs. 60 lakhs and export facilities was also included. Henceforth their investment limit was raised to Rs.95 lakhs on condition that they would export 30% of their output. As per the industrial policy resolution 1996 to 1997, the investment again increased to Rs. 3 crores from Rs. 95 lakhs. In 1999-2000 the said limit in investment was reduced to Rs. 1 crore from Rs. 3 crores.

Objectives of the Study

1. The objectives of the study have been highlighted to measure the growth of SSI in Orissa during 10 years, i.e. 1991-92 to 2000-01.
2. To evaluate the reasons of sickness of the industries.
3. To establish the relation between investment and number of units engaged; investment and employment by applying spearman's rank correlation.
4. To measure the amount of advances sanctioned and their achievements by various financial institutions in the field of economy of the country.

Methodology of the Study

1. The secondary data relating to SSI of Orissa have been collected from the "Statistics wing of Directorate of Industries, Cuttack, Orissa.
2. The advances sanctioned by various financial institution for (only) five year have been collected from state level Banking committee, Bhubaneswar, Orissa.
3. The study is undertaken with the following sub-heads;
   (a) Introduction of SSI
   (b) Growth of small-scale industries in Orissa.
   (c) Financial Assistance to SSI in Orissa.
   (d) Conclusions and suggestions.
4. A Null-Hypothesis has been assumed under this study that there has not been any association or relation between investment and number of units established investment and employment in SSI in Orissa.

Limitations of the Study

1. Due to non-availability of data relating to financial assistances by various institution for 10 years the complete picture of SSI units could not be drawn.
2. The information relating to productions and sales of various industries have not been availed from the "static wing of Directorate of Industries, Cuttack, Orissa.

Growth of Small-Scale Industries in Orissa

Orissa is enriched with minerals, forest and agricultural products. As per history of Orissa, there are so many artisians who reveals their skill and knowledge in the field of art and culture through temples like Konark and Lord Jagannath.

After the industrial revolution in India, every state adopted such policy to make establish the small scale industries in their own state. Orissa is also one of them. It is controlled and guided by Director of Industries, Cuttack, Orissa under the ministry of industries. At first it had 17 districts industrial centre in the state. Again due to the reorganisation of districts it was converted into 31 units. Besides there are 12 categories of industries such as Food and Allied, Chemical and Allied, Electrical and Electronics, Engineering and Metal Based, Forest and Wood Based, Glass and Ceramic Based, Live Stock and Leather Based, Paper and Paper products, Rubber and Plastics, Textiles, Miscellaneous Manufacturing, Repairing and Servicing found in it.

Table—14.1

Year	*No. of Units*	*Investment (Rs. in lakhs)*	*Employment*	*Advance received (Rs. in lakhs)*
1	2	3	4	5
91-92	**2233**	**5203.38**	**15,545**	
92-93	**2117**	**5499.96 (5.7%)**	**13,344**	
93-94	**2311**	**5620.64 (2.2%)**	**13,807**	
94-95	**2327**	**6808.15 (21.12%)**	**13,096**	

(Table Contd...)

1	2	3	4	5
95-96	2507	7481.90 (9.9%)	13.019	
96-97	3098	10452.52 (39.7%)	15.629	12407.54
97-98	3186	13408.70 (28.28%)	16,716	15935.09
98-99	3184	19006.28 (41.71%)	16,776	17352.27
99-2000	3519	15480.24 (-18.55%)	18,578	17038.00
2000-01	3678	15317.64 (-1.05%)	18,115	19868.71
Average	2861.49	9487.94	15462.5	

Source: Directorate of Industries, Cuttack, Orissa.

Analysis and Interpretation

As per table-14.1 under the study, it is found that there are 28,615 numbers of small-scale units during the periods 1991-92 to 2000-01. The numbers of units have been increased in a progressing ways besides the year 1992-93 and 1998-99. Moreover there has been a spectacular achievement in the year 1996-97 showing an increase 23.5% than that of the previous year. So the new industrial resolution policy has been properly followed. Similarly another achievement has been earmarked in the year 1999-2000 showing an increase of (24.87%) than that of the year 1998-99 which indicates that new policy initiatives in the year 1999-2000, it is marked by that average investment during the ten years is Rs. 9487.94 lakhs.

That the investment of Rs. 19006.28 lakhs have been the highest amount in the year 1998-99 followed by Rs. 15,480.24 lakhs, Rs. 15,317.64 lakhs, Rs. 13,408.70 lakh and Rs. 10,452-52.52 lakhs during the years 1999-2000, 00-01, 1997-98 and 1996-97 respectively. From the above study, it reveals that in spite of increase of investment and availability of Bank's loans, the numbers of units have not been geared in comparison to the previous years for the cause of modernisation and installation of plant and machinery. Moreover during the years 1991 to 1996, the investments positions of the respective categories of industries have been enlisted less than the average investment under the study which indicates an adoption of new global policy faced by SSI in Orissa. Similarly from the point of view of employments, the average employment under the study has been calculated as 15,462.5 whereas highest employment is marked as 18,578 in the year 1999-2000 followed by to 18,115, 16,776, 16,716, 15,729, 15,545 during the years 2000-01, 1998-99, 1997-98, 1996-97 and 1991-92 respectively. Again considering the progress of employment, it is found that there has been a decline rate of growth during the periods 1992-93 to 1995-96 after the liberalisation of policy by Govt. of India.

As per the table - 2 it indicates that there has been a tremendous growth of SSI in India from the point of view of number of units and employment. But it is felt that there has not been any upward trend of SSI in Orissa.

Spearman's Rank Correlation Between Investment and Number of Units

An attempt has been made by taking a null hypothesis that there is not any correlation among investments and number of units engaged; investment and employment in SSI of Orissa. By looking the spearman's rank correlation from the table-14.1 it is found that rank correlation coefficient is 0.94 whereas the critical table value as per appendix table-14.7 marked = 0.6364 at 5% level of significance. Henceforth the above study rejects null-hypothesis as the calculated value is more than table value. So it indicates that there has been a positive association between investment and number of units engaged in SSI.

Table—14.2 Overall Performance of SSI Sector in India

Year	*No. of Units (in lakhs)*	*Employment (in lakhs)*
1	2	3
1991-92	20.82	129.80
1992-93	22.46	134.06
1993-94	23.81	139.38
1994-95	25.71	146.56

(Table Contd...)

1	2	3
1995-96	27.24	152.61
1996-97	28.57	160.00
1997-98	30.14	167.20
1998-99	31.21	171.58(p)

Sources: Economic survey–1999-2000, p. 126.

Besides it is also further noticed that the investment and number of units engaged in the year 1998-99 have occupied the best rank during the study period.

Similarly in case of investment and employment, rank correlation is 0.74. But the table at .20 level of significance as per appendix table—7 is 0.4424 which indicates lower than calculated value. Hence the null hypothesis is rejected and it shows that there have been a positive correlation towards investment and employment. From the angle of ranking of investment and employment, the years 1998-99 and 1999-2000 have occupied the first and second position respectively.

Institutional Finance to SSI Sector

In India various financial institutions are established to assist various sector of the economy. At present, there are 12 institutions at national level and 46 state level. The all Indian Financial Institutions comprise 6 All India Development banks namely; I.D.B.I, I.F.C.I, ICICI, SIDBI, IRBI, and SCICI. Beside these, there are 3 investment institutions such as L.I.C, G.I.C and U.T.I.

From the angle of financing of SSI in Orissa, financial institutions such as Nationalised Banks, Co-operative Banks, Urban Co-operative Banks and OSFC play very vital role. As per the aforesaid institutions, OSFC assist measure portions of financial help to SSI of Orissa.

Table—14.3 Advanced Sanctioned and Disbursed by Nationalised Banks, Co-operative Banks, Urban Co-operative Banks and OSFC in Orissa

Year	*Target (Rs. in Lakhs)*	*Achievement (Rs. in Lakhs)*
1996-97	19,157.15	12,407.54
1997-98	18,503.35	15,935.09
1998-99	20,678.00	17,352.27
1999-2000	21,116.00	17,038.00
2000-2001	26,411.33	19,868.71

Sources: SLBC, Bhubaneswar, Orissa.

On considering the Table—14.3, it is found that there have been increasing rate of sanctions by financial institutions during the periods ranging from 1996-97 to 2000-01 under the study. Similarly from the point of view of achievement, it is marked that there has been spectacular achievement in the year 1997-98 (86.12% of sanctions) by financial institutions. Again there have been very low rate of achievements during the periods i.e. 1996-97 (64.67%) and 2000-01 (75.22%). So the above study indicates that the financial institutions are reluctant to disburse the amount for the development of SSI in Orissa.

Table—14.4 Terms Loan Sanctioned and Disbursed to SSI Units by OSFC

(Rs. in lakhs)

Year	*Target*	*Disbursement*
1991-92	1983.35	2190.66 (7th plan)
1992-93	2683.04	2165.79 (8th plan)
1993-94	2114.41	2529.34
1994-95	1596.27	1894.87
1995-96	2749.86	2052.61
1996-97	3204.36	3136.39
1997-98	5598.60	2811.32
1998-99	4374.22	2560.47
1999-2000	NA	4790.00
2000-2001	5686.01	5408.10

Sources: OSFC, Cuttack, Orissa.

Table—14.4 witnesses the sanctions and disbursements by OSFC, Cuttack according to the 7th, 8th and 9th Five Year Plan. For that point of view, excess disbursement than sanctions have been shown in few years. Comparing that Table—14.3 and Table—14.4, it is calculated that OSFC has disbursed loans more than 25% of other financial institutions. So OSFC has contributed its stringent efforts towards the SSI units in Orissa for the progress of the economy of the country.

Suggestions

1. The Govt. of Orissa should increase the number of units of small sectors by creating more opportunities as it has achieved target only 0.11% of the number of units of the whole country.
2. In regards to employment, it is achieved only 0.10% of the whole economy. So the SSI of Orissa should enhance their production capacity as well as creation of more markets so that unemployment problems would be solved.
3. The Govt. of Orissa would arrange proper training for the development of entrepreneurship.
4. In view of global competition, SSI sector should keep their mind for producing qualitative goods.
5. From the angle of advances, the financial institutions should provide funds adequately without any bottlenecks.
6. The Govt. of Orissa should be vigilant in regard to SSI sectors management of the business and prevailing labour unrest.

15

Institutional Financing for Small Scale Industrial Development in Orissa

Bhagabata Behera*

Introduction

Institutional agencies have played a significant role in the development of industries in particular and economic growth of the nation in general. They also have contributed significantly in reducing regional imbalances and development of backward regions. The industrialisation and growth of the industries include growth of large scale industries, medium scale industries and small scale industries. The small industries (SSI) sector in India has, over the last five decades played significant role in building a strong and stable national economy. It is one of the largest employers in the country providing direct employment to an estimated of over 17 million persons and thus meeting key objective of providing employment, facilitating regional dispersal of industrial units and earning foreign exchange. So the Government of India has been assigning increasing emphasis on the development of small scale industries through various policy measures adopted from time to time.

* **Jr. Lecture in Commerce, Bhadrak College, Bhadrak.**

In almost all the state of our country, the small scale industries have a very significant role. In Orissa, these industries have a major share in industrial growth. Orissa having all potential to become a leading industrial state in the country has remained backward. This state in particular has everything these are needed for industrialisation. Industrious human power is found in every corner of the state. The state has abundant mineral resources, surplus power, improved distribution system and reasonable power tariff. The political situation is relatively stable. But it has poor road and telecom network limited reach of railways, low rate of literacy, poor health coverage and low infrastructural facilities for attracting entrepreneurs for establishing industry. So the state is in the urgent needs of infrastructure finance and marketing management. Both of these needs huge capital investment, various financial institution has been trying their best to boost the industrial growth of the state by providing various long-term and short-term finance under various schemes. However small scale industries has failed in achieving its objective during the course of its operation. So it has become necessary to study the role of financial institution in financing for small scale industrial development of Orissa.

With this backdrop of industrial growth and their financing scenario, in this paper an attempt has been made to evaluate the institutional financing for small scale industrial development of Orissa.

Sources of Data

The data used in the study are mainly collected from secondary sources.

Importance and Objective of the Study

Finance is the lifeblood of every business and no business can move a step without finance. The activities of all sections of the society starting from beggars to the mega industrialist of the country are moulded by financial factor.

The vital needs of finance is doubly realised when it is a case of the small industry. Every problem of the small produced ranging from production of material to marketing is, in the ultimate analysis, a financial one. Adequate finance is a pre-requisite for proper organisation of production and disposal of product in the market. One of the biggest hurdles on the growth of SSIs is the non-availability of cheap finance. It is also viewed as a principal constraint on the ability of the entrepreneur to initiate and upgrade. Inadequate finance is the major constraint on the operation, maintenance and growth of small scale industries.

Considering the need of finance, the SSIs require them for two purposes.

1. To invest in long term productive assets like purchase of land and building, plant and machinery, furniture and fixture etc. This constitutes the fixed capital requirement of the units.
2. To meet all short term expenditure like purchase of raw material payment of wages and other day to day financial needs. This comprises the working capital of the SSIs.

However the need of working capital is more pressing than the initial fixed investment and enables a small units to maintain a sound credit system, avoid insolvency, take advantages of cash discount enables to strike profitable bargain in transaction carry out expansion programmes and undertake research and innovation.

Objectives

The present study proposes to analyse the role of various financial institutions in the growth and development in respect of SSI in the following points.

1. To present a brief panorama of the small scale industries (SSIs) of the state of Orissa in relation to growth of employment with that of the investment.
2. To evaluate the role of the leading financial institution. OSFC as a major sources in providing financial assistance for the development of SSI in the state.
3. To analyse the amount of advance sanctioned and disbursed by the OSFC to different type of industries.
4. To analyse the role of the state Govt. in providing finance and subsidy to SSIs in Orissa.

Growth of Small Scale Industries in Orissa

The growth of small scale industries in Orissa was not in a remarkable stage. The Government of Orissa undertaking various incentive measure lie infrastructure development, improve industrial climate, assistance to export-oriented units, incentive for employment, different measure for restructuring sick units, excise duty concessions, provision for raw materials, marketing support, facilities for technology upgradation and also trying to mobilise resources from abroad. In spite of all these efforts, the industrial climate has not witnessed a remarkable shift. The table-15.1 show the growth of small scale industries in Orissa.

Table—15.1 Growth of Small Scale Industries in Orissa

Year	*No. of SSI set up*	*Investment Rs. in crores*	*Investment per unit in lakh*	*Employment (nos.)*	*Employment per unit*
By the end of the7th Plan	35845	435.57	1.2	265286	7.4
1990-91	2249	61.00	2.7	15657	7.0
1991-92	2233	52.03	2.3	15545	7.0
During 8th plan	12360	358.63	2.9	68895	5.57
1997-98	3186	134.06	4.2	16716	5.2
1998-99	3184	190.06	6.0	16776	5.3
1999-2000	3473	162.94	4.7	18608	5.35
2000-2001	3676	15318	4.1	18115	4.9
Total	66206	1574.5	2.37	435598	6.57

Source: Directorate of Industries Govt. of Orissa, Cuttack

If we analyse the table-15.1 the growth pattern of small scale industries in the state. It is found that just after the seventh five year plan the number as new units are going on increasing excepting the year 1992-93. During the 8th plan onwards, it is in a remarkable stage. Investment in the units from beginning is revealing a marginal rise per units. In 1997-98, 1998-99 the investment in units is in a remarkable stage, but at the same time the employment generation is indicating a negative trend per unit. From the emerging trend it may be concluded irrespective of all financial and infrastructural incentives the employment system has no positive impact with increasing numbers of new units. During 1999-2000 and 2000-2001 the investment units show a decreasing trend.

Shortage of finance is one of the major problems for the small scale units. The financial institutions are called upon to play a major role in providing finance to small scale industries. But the share of institutional finance in the total investment is less in the case of small scale enterprises compared to large industries. The second report of the international prospective planning team observed that considering the vital role of small industries, the total amount of loan granted to small industries, forms a small part of the total loans to industrial sector of the country.

All India financial institutions even have been continuously trying to provide adequate financial assistance to the industries in Orissa. They have offered risk capital, venture capital and technological finance. SIDBI, OSFC and commercial banks are providing finance to SSIs under various schemes.

The leading financial institution, OSFC is trying its best in accelerating the industrial growth of the state by providing varieties of long term finance under different schemes.

From Table-15.2 it is observed that there is an irregular growth in financing of small scale units from 7th five year plan the loans sanctioned to SSIs are going on increasing. During 8th five year plan in the year of 1994-95 the lowest percent of loan is sanctioned to SSI. Highest percentage is sanctioned in the year 1997-98. But in 1998-99 it is seen that there is a decrease in the amount of loan sanctioned. As for as the sanction to numbers of SSI unit is concerned, there is a decreasing trend which is not admirable. It is observed that the numbers of SSI units getting loan from OSFC is gradually decreasing. It is further expected to fall in future.

From the sanction and disbursement point of view there is increased trend of the percentage of disbursement, in accordance to sanction. But from the year of 1997-98 and 1998-99 it is seen that there is a decrease trend. Though highest amount of loan is sanctioned in 1997-98 but the disbursement is quite low.

Table—15.2 Term Loan Sanctioned and Disbursed to SSI Units by OSFC During Different Plan Periods

(Rs. in lakh)

Period	*Sanction*			*Disbursement*			*Percentage*
	Number	*Amount*	*Per unit*	*Number*	*Amount*	*Per unit*	
By the end of 1979-80	6114	4366.28	0.7	3605	2726.90	0.75	62.45
During 6th five year plan	23682	19883.54	0.8	10685	13097.39	1.22	65.87
During 7th five year plan	4549	16660.64	3.6	1930	16017.58	8.3	96.00
1990-91	456	2729.33	6.0	170	2650.98	15.6	97.00
1991-92	299	1983.55	6.6	258	2190.66	8.5	110.40
During 8th five year plan	1016	12347.94	12.15	1089	11779.00	10.8	95.40
1997-98	357	5598.60	15.7	279	2811.32	10.0	50.00
1998-99	312	4374.22	14.0	197	2560.47	13.0	58.50
Grand total	**36785**	**67944.10**	**1.8**	**18231**	**53834.30**	**2.9**	**79.20**

Source: OSFC, Cuttack.

From Table-15.3 it is evident that the maximum amount has been disbursed to the district especially to Cuttack, Puri, Khurda, Ganjam and Sundargarh and Koraput. Maximum amount of disbursement is made in Cuttack and Sundargarh in comparison to sanction. Khurda and Sambalpur have got less disbursement than the sanction. Whereas in Baragarh the disbursement is zero. There is no sanction and disbursement in the district like Sonepur and Nuapada and Nowarangpur. The amount of disbursement to newly created district is very low. Further the corporation has so far, concentrated its attention on the development of a few advance district only. The performance of OSFC in respect of small scale industrial growth of backward district is not upto the expectations. There are many reasons behind it. The government policy varies from time to time which has influenced the financing of industrial units. There is no rational and consistent policy of Govt. for which the instant steps might have encouraged or discouraged the setting up of or financing the units. Secondly the per unit sanctioned amount show gradual and consistent growth rate. It might be possible because of inflationary trend.

Table—15.3 District Wise Investment (Block Capital/Working Capital) Break Up of SSI Units Up During 1998-99

(Rs. in lakh)

District code	*District Name*	*Number of SSI units set-up*	*Capital invested*		
			Block	*Working*	*Total*
1	2	3	4	5	6
1.	Angul	140	165.44	64.30	229.74
2.	Balasore	192	156.16	137.84	594.00
3.	Bargarh	110	574.48	143.82	718.30
4.	Bhadrak	84	146.34	63.30	209.64
5.	Bolangir	95	386.87	196.87	583.74
6.	Boudh	15	75.33	31.44	106.77
7.	Cuttack	257	3208.34	1538.21	4746.55
8.	Deogarh	15	13.41	4.79	18.20
9.	Dhenkanal	81	90.77	30.51	121.28

(Table Contd...)

1	2	3	4	5	6
10.	Gajapati	51	94.57	56.96	151.53
11.	Ganjam	224	1368.98	383.10	1752.08
12.	Jagatsinghpur	85	77.61	18.56	96.17
13.	Jajpur	142	610.99	86.69	697.68
14.	Jharsuguda	49	96.39	30.77	127.16
15.	Kalahandi	56	442.07	94.63	536.00
16.	Kandhmal	51	50.59	4.10	54.69
17.	Kendrapara	72	138.08	24.74	162.82
18.	Keonjhar	112	865.06	128.69	993.75
19.	Khurda	243	1399.59	394.33	1793.92
20.	Koraput	100	347.76	145.19	492.95
21.	Malkangiri	26	30.05	5.45	35.50
22.	Mayurbhanj	166	292.62	91.53	384.15
23.	Nawapara	21	65.61	4.69	70.30
24.	Nawarangpur	45	105.81	38.57	144.38
25.	Nayagarh	53	116.52	38.42	154.94
26.	Puri	104	529.80	29.30	559.10
27.	Rayagada	98	389.06	130.38	519.44
28.	Sambalpur	80	159.41	91.49	250.90
29.	Sonepur	38	41.56	9.34	50.90
30.	Sundargarh	379	2043.45	605.53	2648.98
	Total	**3184**	**14382.72**	**4623.54**	**19006.26**

The OSFC is giving maximum priority to medium and large scale units.

From Table-15.1 it is observed that the setting up of new units are not impressive. No linear relationship is observed between investment, number of units and employment generation. The emerging trend reveals that the industrial units after introduction of new economic policy (1991) have been more capital-intensive with innovative technology. With introduction of new technology and modernisation programme there is no positive impact on generation of further employment. The growth of units and employment generation have not commensurate to each other.

From Table-15.4 it is observed that the maximum preference is given to chemical industrial units, metal manufacturing units, food manufacturing units. Whereas the investment in paper industries, leather based industries, Textile, forest and wood based industries is very low. Textile units is highly neglected. The employment generation in relating to investment per unit is acceptable.

Table—15.4 Sanction and Disbursement of State Investment Subsidy to Small Scale Industries

(Rs. in lakh)

Year	*Sanction*		*Disbursement*	
	Number	*Amount*	*Number*	*Amount*
1989-90	261	257.12	348	213.53
1990-91	268	298.83	–	–
1991-92	250	356.08	562	489.45
1992-93	372	439.41	356	435.72
1993-94	182	253.11	281	292.19
1994-95	113	144.07	48	53.17
1995-96	91	156.90	103	119.11
1996-97	154	485.91	457	663.76
1997-98	143	346.06	268	471.01
1998-99	132	439.41	50	162.16
Total	**1966**	**3176.90**	**2473**	**2900.12**

Source: OSFC, Cuttack.

From Table-15.4 it is observed that the state investment subsidy to small scale industries is not impressive. The number of sick units are increasing due to lack of finance, several sick units have expressed that the dearth of needed capital is the main reason for the resulting incipient sickness. There is also insufficient and improper transfer of financial resources from center to the state. An analysis of the year-wise sanction and disbursement of the state investment subsidy to number of SSI shows a decreasing trend. In the year of 1990-91 there is no disbursement. In the year 1998-99 the disbursement to number of industry is very low.

The investment in block capital and also in working capital is very low. Working capital is provided by the commercial bank. The finance provided by SIDBI is insufficient. The financial health of maximum financial institutions are not sound. The amount of NPA (non-performing assets) increasing day by day in the balance sheet of commercial bank. They should be more careful while sanctioning the loans to SSI. A timely follow-up measure can avoid the chances of bad debts by any unit. Again the recovery department must be more active. They have to collect the money in due time so that there will be no outstanding amount of balance for a long period.

Conclusion

The development of small scale industries in Orissa has so far been at dismally low level due to several reasons like lack of inadequate infrastructural facilities, problem of finance, marketing etc. The financial institutions are not functioning in proper way. A large number of new entrepreneurs are having bitter experience of complying to long and varied legal formalities following the pre-credit sanction procedure of financial institutions in the state. It is noticed that the entrepreneurs are often delayed and unduly harassed before the financial sanction. This procedural delay in sanction of financial assistance of the existing system may be reviewed by the government and liberal credit sanction policy may be introduced in order to enroll more and more number of entrepreneurs in small scale sector.

From the financing working capital point of view the present credit flow of the organized financial institution to the small scale industrial sector is exposed to serious constraints in regarding to working capital. Compared to capital goods, the working capital requirement is a subject to greater escalations in account of domestic market inflation. Any hike in price the domestic market affects adversely. The marginal capacity of production of industries from the experience it is observed that new project and new entrepreneurs do not with-stand to such domestic inflationary pressure and suffer from financial crises so much so that they fail to put their factories in to operation and thus go sick and it has an adverse impact in the volume of credit recovery by the financial institution which again has serious implications on their liquidity position.

So the government should initiate policies to facilitate the new entrepreneurs to avail easy term credit for additional working capital requirement. Again the government should initiate action to enrich domestic entrepreneurial talent through training, seminars conferences etc. In the last but not least it has become a joint responsibility of government, research institutions and financial institutions to think seriously about emerging trend of industrial growth and their financing in Orissa.

REFERENCES

1. *Small Scale Industries and India's Economic Development*, Deep and Deep Publication, New Delhi.
2. *Statistical Hand Book of Small Scale Industries 1998-99*, Directorate of Industries Orissa, Cuttack.
3. OSFC Annual Repots.
4. Economic Survey of Orissa.

16

Disparity in Institutional Financing for Small Scale Industrial Development of Orissa

A Study of OSFC

Dr. Bhagaban Das*

Introduction

Attention towards regional disparities in India is not recent origin. Only during last twenty to thirty years, the planners have started giving attention to this problem. One of the objective of the sixth plan framework of India is, "A progressive reduction in regional inequalities in the pace of development and in the diffusion of technological benefits, the planners are conscious of the fact that planning in the course of the last five decades has not been conducive to balanced industrial and economic development of the country.

The main objectives of the State Financial Corporations (SFCs) are to achieve balanced regional growth, generate employment, catalyse investment and widen the ownership base of industries. They have been playing a pioneering role in the promotion and development of small and medium industries in their respective states. In spite of this, there are disparities in the institutional

* **Senior Faculty, P.G. Department of Commerce, Dhenkanal College, Dhenkanal.**

financing not only between one state to another, but also among various regions of the same state. In Orissa, the problem of the regional imbalance in institutional financing is more serious in nature. Poverty, exploitation, subsistence living and unemployment are evident in backward and non-coastal Orissa. It projects extreme regional variation in terms financing to small scale industries, for instance, it was found in ___ "out of three regions of Orissa, two are unable to get their legitimate claim even at the end of March, 2000". So it is clear that within a state, some regions get higher amount of institutional finance, whereas others lack it.

Objective of the Study

Under these circumstances, an attempt has been made to determine the extent and magnitude of regional disparity that exits in institutional finance with regard to small-scale industries financed by Orissa State Financial Corporation during the period of 1997 to 2000.

Methodology

The study is mainly confined to disparity in institutional financing in SSI units financed by OSFC. During the period of study, 1394 small-scale industrial units were financed with an amount of Rs.17187.53 lakhs by the Corporation. All these 1394 units have been taken in the study to compare and analyses the nature and depth of regional disparities in institutional financing. The data for the study have been collected from the original official records of OSFC; Head Office, Cuttack and Branch office, Dhenkanal. The data so collected are analysed on the basis of certain statistical techniques and are presented in different formats for the convenience of the study.

Hypothesis for the Study

The study, broadly aims at examining the following hypothesis with the use of data.

(a) OSFC gives greater emphasis in the development of SSI units.

(b) Small Scale Industries development in backward districts is slower than the non-backward districts.

(c) OSFC accentuates regional imbalance in small-scale industries financing.

II

ORISSA STATE FINANCIAL CORPORATION AND SMALL SCALE INDUSTRIAL UNITS

OSFC is necessarily a promotional and financing agency. It provides assistance to small-scale industries medium scale industries, small road transport operation and others. The ratio of sanction to small-scale units the corporation out of total sanction is not encouraging.

Table—16.1 Percentage of Loan Sanctioned to SSI Units

Year	*Percentage of the SSI units to total units*	*Percentage of loan sanctioned to SSI unit to total amount*
1989-90	51	52
1990-91	39	55
1991-92	29	40
1992-93	29	49
1993-94	23	41
1994-95	24	41
1995-96	18	33
1996-97	22	28
1997-98	52	47
1998-99	64	45
1999-2k	41	55

Computed from different Annual Reports of OSFC.

In the table-16.1, we find that in 1989-90, the percentage of number of units in small-scale industries to total units was 51. But from 1990-91 and onwards we observe the percentage has gone down drastically. In 1995-96, it has gone down to 18 per cent only. In 1997-98 and 1998-99 it gone up to 52 per cent and 64 per cent respectively which is abnormal, because it again showed a declining trend in 1999-2000, i.e. 41 per cent. In 1998-99 total number units of loan sanctioned was 1527, out of which it was 785 to SSI units. But in 1995-96 it was only 180 out of 1014 units. In 1989-90, the total amount of loan sanctioned was Rs. 58.38 crores, out of which

Rs. 31.38 crore were advanced to small-scale industries. It is 52 per cent of total amount. In 1993-94 it came to 41 per cent, which is Rs.15.96 crores out of Rs. 38.68 crores. In subsequent two years the proportion gone down to 33 per cent and 28 per cent. So after liberalisation, the small-scale industrial sector have been neglected in number and also in amount. However, the last two years of our study showed a revival of its previous trend.

In table-16.2, the situation we observe is not different from table-16.1. The actual disbursement of loan to small-scale industries has decreased year after year. It was 71 per cent of total disbursement in 1989-90. But from 1990-91 onwards, the proportion declined and it reached to an all time low of 28 per cent in 1997-98. On the number basis, the SSI units also shows a declining trend.

Table—16.2 Percentage of Loan Disbursed to SSI Units

Year	*% of actual disbursement of loan to SSI to total loan*	*% of loan to SSI unit in number to total units*
1989-90	71	38
1990-91	53	23
1991-92	43	26
1992-93	44	30
1993-94	55	26
1994-95	54	31
1995-96	38	26
1996-97	33	26
1997-98	28	24
1998-99	48	43
1999-2k	37	41

Computed from Annual Reports of OSFC.

III

Orissa is a backward state so for as industry is concerned. In the state there are some districts which are known as backward and there are some districts, which are non-backward. In order to have an idea of the importance accorded to development of backward districts, the amount sanctioned and number of units assisted are shown under these two heads in Table–16.3. Of the 13 undivided districts of the state, 8 have been identified as backward. These include the undivided Balasore, Koraput, Kalahandi, Dhenkanal, Keonjhar, Mayurbhanja, Bolangir, and Phulbani. It is one of the policy major under the Industrial Policy of the state government to promote industries in backward areas to remove the regional disparity. OSFC being one of the financing agencies of the state government has the objective to look after this policy. As a policy matter, the corporation takes this matter as a special objective.

Table—16.3 Amount of Loan Sanctioned to Backward and Non-Backward Districts

(Rs. crores)

Year	*Backward Districts*			*Non-Backward Districts*		
	Amount	*% on total*	*Trend*	*Amount*	*% on total*	*Trend*
1986-87	20.26	40	100	30.39	60	100
1987-88	19.35	41	95.50	27.84	59	91.69
1988-89	22.27	34	110.09	43.23	696	91.59
1989-90	18.24	31	90.02	45.20	69	142.22
1990-91	15.73	32	77.70	33.42	68	148.71
1991-92	–	–	–	–	–	–
1992-93	13.21	24	65.25	41.83	76	137.62
1993-94	14.95	28	73.85	38.44	72	126.47
1994-95	11.83	31	41.07	26.33	69	86.63
1995-96	24.65	29	121.73	60.35	71	198.55
1996-97	33.59	29	165.91	82.23	71	270.53
1997-98	17.36	31	85.78	38.62	69	127.06
1998-99	12.59	29	62.19	31.15	71	102.46
1999-2k	16.91	24	83.53	55.24	76	181.73

Source: Different Annual Reports of OSFC

As we analyse the table-16.3, we find an amusing situation. The loan sanctioned to non-backward districts has been maintained. It is in respect of percentage to total loan of OSFC and also in respect of trend of loan. In the year 1992-93, 1993-94, 1996-97 and 1999-2000 this figure is very much encouraging. On the other hand, the situation for backward districts is totally different. The amount of loan has gone down drastically. In the year 1986-87, the amount of loan was Rs.20.26 crores and in 1998-89 it raise to Rs.22.27 crores. But after 1988-89, the situation changed. The amount of loan slipped to Rs.11.83 in 1994-95. The percentage of this loan to total loan amount has also come down from 40 in 1986-87 to 24 in 1999-2000, from this, it is clear that attention to non-backward areas is properly maintained, whereas backward districts are neglected during the period of our study.

Table—16.4 Quotients for Sanction of Loan by OSFC

Year	*1980-81*	*1984-85*	*1989-90*	*1997-98*	*1998-99*	*1999-2000*
Backward Districts	0.59	0.60	0.68	0.65	0.60	0.49
Non-Backward Districts	1.37	1.37	1.29	1.32	1.36	1.47

These quotients for sanctions have been computed for the backward and non-backward districts in relation to the share of the population of these districts. The share of population of 8 backward districts was 47.76 per cent as against 52.24 per cent in the non-backward districts. The value suggests that, even by 2000, the backward districts did not get their legitimate share despite the higher rate of growth of sanctions. It is also evident that the backward districts were affected perceptibly during the last year of the study, ending 31st, March 2000. When the quotient declined to all time low of 0.49 only. It indicates that these districts have only got half of their legitimate share of sanctions. On the other hand, the non-backward districts' quotient shows an increasing trend. It was 1.37 in 1980-81 and gradually increased and reached at 1.47 by the end of March 2000. That means, these districts has received the sanction of all most one and half times of their original share due, at the cost of the backward districts.

For the purpose of our study the whole Orissa is divided into three broad classifications, such as (i) coastal Orissa, which contains the district of Cuttack, Puri, Balasore and Ganjam, (ii) Western Orissa consists of the districts, like Sambalpur, Sundargarh, Bolangir, Koraput and Kalahandi and rest is under the head Rest of Orissa group. The quotients for the regions of Coastal Orissa worked out to be 1.03, 1.02 and 1.36 and 0.89 for western Orissa and 0.58, 0.32 and 0.62 for the rest of the Orissa during the same period. It

IV

Table—16.5 Regional Analysis of Sanctions (Amount in crores)

Year	*1997-98*			*1998-99*			*1999-2000*		
Region	*Unit%*	*Amount%*	*Quotient*	*Unit%*	*Amount%*	*Quotient*	*Unit%*	*Amount%*	*Quotient*
Coastal	45.38	49.05	1.03	50.96	48.54	1.02	71.17	58.58	1.23
Western	43.98	39.92	1.19	40.06	45.40	1.36	17.80	29.71	0.89
Rest of Orissa	38.00	11.03	0.58	8.98	6.06	0.32	11.03	11.71	0.62
Orissa	100	100	1	100	100	1	100	100	1

suggests that the later two regions did not get their due share in the total sanctions by the corporation. Since coastal Orissa is industrially developed except Balasore district, there is no justification for a higher share for it in the total assistance. So, we can conclude that though the corporation rendered financial assistance on a large scale, the non-coastal regions did not get their due shares.

Testing of Hypothesis

As mentioned earlier, we have examined the following hypotheses in this study.

1. OSFC Gives Greater Emphasis for the Development of SSI Units

This hypothesis has been examined after taking into account the percentage of assistance sanctioned to SSI units to total amount as well as percentage of SSI units assisted total number of units. In 1989-90, the percentage number of units, in small-scale industries to total units was 51. But it reduced gradually and touched 18 per cent only in 1996-97. Similarly, the percentage of loan sanctioned was 52 per cent of total amount in 1989-90 and it has also gone down to 28 per cent in 1996-97. So, we can conclude that small-scale industrial sector has been neglected after liberalisation of our economy. Therefore, this hypothesis does not hold good.

2. Small-scale Industries Development in Backward Districts is Slower than the Non-backward Districts

This hypothesis has been examined after taking into account the total assistance sanctioned to the SSI units of different districts by the corporation and by determining the quotients for sanctions of loan. In our study, we found that for non-backward districts, the percentage of loan to SSI units was 60 in 1986-87. But it gradually rises up to 76 in the year 1999-2000. During the same time on the other hand, the backward districts share fall down from 40 per cent to 24 per cent. The quotient value also shows that the backward districts did not get their legitimate claim even by end of March 2000. Therefore, this hypothesis holds good.

3. OSFC Accentuates Regional Imbalance

This hypothesis has been examined after taking into account the total assistance sanctioned by the corporation to different regions of the state. The state is categorised by the three regions for our study, such as; Coastal Orissa, Western Orissa and Rest of Orissa. Costal Orissa's share was 49.05 per cent in the total amount of sanction in 1997-98 and it increased to 58.58 per cent in 1999-2000. During the same period, the share of Western Orissa has gone down from 39.92 per cent to 29.71 per cent; whereas the Rest of Orissa shows almost no change. (i.e. 11.03 to 11.71 per cent). It can be broadly observed from the above analysis that major portion of the total amount has been canalised towards the coastal region throughout the period of our study. Moreover, to support our conclusion we have calculated quotient for sanctions. At the end of March 2000, it stands 1.23 for coastal region, 0.89 for Western region and 0.62 for Rest of Orissa. Thus, it is clear that coastal Orissa gets more assistance than their due share, whereas the other two regions are deprived of their claims. Therefore, we can conclude that the corporation accentuates the regional imbalance. Hence our hypothesis holds good.

REFERENCES

1. Bharati, D. and Das, N.C.; Regional Imbalance "A focus on Northeast Region". *The Indian Journal of Commerce*, Vol. xxxvii, 1984. pp.128-135.
2. "*Economic Survey of Orissa*"; Bureau of Statistics and Economic, Orissa 1994-95, 1997-98.
3. Mahabala, M., "Simplifying Rules and Procedures," *Management Review*, 11 MB, Bangalore, Vol. 9, No.4, October 1997-98.
4. Mohanty, S; - Sixth Plan of Orissa in the Context of Growing Regional Disparity in India - *Orissa Economic Journal* - (Vol. XIII, 1980, p.17.
5. Annual Reports of OSFC.

17

Government of India Policies on SSIs

Prof. P.K. Sahu*

Small industry development has been one of the major planks of Indian economic development strategy since independence in 1947. While going through the policies of the Government on SSIs, the period of last five decades can be broadly divided into two i.e the era of Protection from 1947 to late 1980 and the era of liberalization and competition since early 1999 till date. During the phase of protection, the Government adopted two pronged strategies on SSI growth, i.e. development of supporting institutional infrastructure and provision of protective benefits.

The supporting institutional infrastructure includes the set up of Small Industries Development Organisation (SIDO), Small Industries Service Institutes (SISIs), National Small Industries Corporation (NSIC), Small Industries Development Bank of India (SIDBI), National Institute of Small Industries Extension Training (NISIET), etc at the central level, Directorate of Industries, Small Industries Development Corporation (SIDC), Small Industries Marketing Corporation (SIMC), and State Financial Corporators (SFCs) at the State level and District Industries Centre (DICs) at the district level. These institutions provide varieties of assistance like

* **Vice-Chairman, State Planning Board, Orissa Secretariat, Bhubaneswar.**

technical service, finance, marketing support, research, training, consultancy, entrepreneurship development, etc. for promotion and accelerated growth in the SSI sector. The policies ensuring protection to SSI sector include definition of SSIs for availing official concessions and incentives, concessional finance, fiscal incentives, price preferences, reservation of SSI products for exclusive government purchase, reservation of items for exclusive manufacture in the SSI sector, raw materials and import policy and exemption from licensing and labour policy.[1]

The initiation of economic reforms through industrial and trade liberalization in 1991-92 marked the beginning of a new era for Indian industry. Industrial de-licensing, removal of threshold limits on assets of large enterprises, liberalization of foreign investments policy, expansion of open general licence (OGL) to include raw material, intermediate and capital goods, reductions of customs duties. These developments nullified the protection that had been enjoyed by SSI sector, by its exclusion from industrial licensing and preferential access to imported inputs and capital goods. As a result, SSI now exposed to the competitive environment. To ensure the sustained growth of SSI in the liberalized competitive environment, the Government of India brought out a New Small Scale Industrial Policy in August 1991. "The primary objective of SSI Policy during the nineties is to impart more vitality and growth impetus to the sector to enable it to contribute its mite fully to the economy particularly in terms of growth output, employment and exports. The policy made it clear that henceforth the emphasis would shift from subsidized credit to ensuring an adequate flow of credit to SSI. Thus the development in 1991-92 in terms of trade and industrial liberalization and exclusive SSI policy, signalled the process of ending protective cover to SSI sector. Following new economic policy to cope up with the challenges of liberalization, the Government of India appointed three important committees to make recommendations for the growth of SSIs in the country. First the Expert Committee on small enterprises under the Chairmanship of Abid Hussain submitted its report in January 1997, second, the High Level Committee on Credit to SSIs under the Chairmanship of S.L. Kapoor submitted to RBI in June 1998 and the third study group on the development of small enterprises under the Chairmanship of S.P. Gupta submitted its interim report on 6th July 2000. In tandem with policies of Government of India, a few of the State Governments have also been releasing policy documents on SSIs. Government of Andhra Pradesh released the policy paper in November 1998 and Federation of Karnataka Chamber of Commerce and Industry released a policy paper on SSIs in May 2000.[2] These documents refer to experiences of few countries and models that can be considered for adoption in India. The S.P. Gupta study group recommended for the (i) three tier definition of tinny, small, medium sector, (ii) bring awareness in small industries sector about WTO implication, (iii) single comprehensive law for SSI (iv) continuation of present reservation for SSI sector, (v) hike in investment limit of Rs. 1 to Rs.5 cr. (vi) In case of export oriented SSI units, set up of a corpus fund of Rs. 2000 cr. to provide infrastructure facilities to SSIs, (vii) Setup of Incubation Infrastructure Development Fund with Rs. 1000 crore to encourage technocrat entrepreneur in high-tech industries like electronics, IT, bio-technology, pharmaceuticals, etc. (viii) for better linkage equity investment by large units in SSIs increased from 24 to 49%, FDI be allowed in SSIs, excise exemption on SSI manufactured goods, (ix) enactment of Limited Partnership Act to bring in more risk capital in SSI sector. SAMADHAN scheme for one time settlement of sick SSI units, (x) enhancement of data base for SSI through fresh census, (xi) development of human resource in SSI sector through training, skill up-gradation, new management practices, (xii) a series of fiscal and financial measures and (xiii) higher marketing support to SSI products through price preference, Government purchase, timely release of institutional finance for export orders of SSI units.

On the basis of the recommendations of S.P. Gupta Study Group, Prime Minister A.B. Vajpayee announced a package of measures to strengthen SSI sector on August 30, 2000. These include: (i) Lowering the investment ceiling in plant and machinery for SSI Sector from Rs. 3 cr. to Rs. 1 cr., (ii) Limit of Composite Loan to SSI units raised from Rs. 10 lakhs to Rs.25 lakhs which include both term loan and working-capital from same agency, (iii) Priority Lending to industry related services and business enterprise with a maximum investment of maximum Rs. 10 lakhs, (iv) Capital subsidy of 12% on investment in technology in selected sectors, (v) Conduct of fresh census to increase the data base for SSI sector, (vi) To continue the grant of Rs.75000 to SSI units opting for ISO 9000 certification for quality management, (vii) Increase of Excise Duty Limit from Rs. 50 lakhs to Rs. 1 cr. to improve the competitive strength of SSIs units, (viii) Group to recommend ways and means to streamline frequent inspection of SSI units by multiple agencies, and (ix) Announcement of Deendayal Hathkarga Protsahan Yojana for Handloom Sector. The Karnataka Chambers of Commerce and Industry also recommended policy shift from control to self regulation strategy, single legislation for SSI sector, cluster approach by locating a group of SSI in specific industrial belts for obtaining necessary infrastructure like finance, tools room facility, packaging, labeling, technology up-gradation facilities quality certification at one place and easy access to institutional credit and working capital at reasonable rates of interests.

REFERENCES

1. Bala Subramanya M.H. 'Shifts in Indians Small Industry Policy', *National Bank News Review*, Vol. 15, No. 3 NABARD, Mumbai, July-Sept. 1999, pp. 27-37.
2. Nagayya D & K.V.'Small Scale Industries: Challenges & Strategies in the Liberalisation Period' *SBI Monthly Review*, Vol. XXXIX, No. 7, Mumbai, July 2000, pp 346-365.